Pilgrimage to Priesthood

Pilgrimage to Priesthood

Elizabeth Canham

First published in Great Britain 1983
SPCK
Holy Trinity Church
Marylebone Road
London NW1 4DU

PUBLISHER'S ACKNOWLEDGEMENTS

Biblical quotations are from the Revised Standard Version of the Bible, copyrighted 1946, 1952 © 1971, 1973 by the Division of Christian Education of the National Council of the Churches of Christ in the USA, and are used by permission.

Extracts from *A Priest Forever* by Carter Heyward are reprinted by permission of Harper & Row.

Extracts from 'Canadian Churchman' (April 1982) are reprinted by permission of the publishers.

The prayer by Charles de Foucauld is reprinted from *The God Who Comes* by Carlo Carretto, published by Darton, Longman & Todd.

Poems by Colin O'Brien Winter are used by permission.

Cover photograph: John Richardson

British Library Cataloguing in Publication Data

Canham, Elizabeth
  Pilgrimage to priesthood.
  1. Canham, Elizabeth   2. Church of England—
  Women clergy—Biography
  I. Title
  283'092'4   BX5199.C/
  ISBN 0-281-04049-4

Typeset by Pioneer, East Sussex
Printed in Great Britain by
Whitstable Litho Ltd, Whitstable, Kent

Dedicated
to the memory of

Colin O'Brien Winter

who sang the Lord's song
in a strange land

Contents

Acknowledgements   viii

Foreword   ix

1   Surprised by Joy   1

2   Let the Women Keep Silence . . .   9

3   The Ministry of Reconciliation   20

4   Kaleidoscope   30

5   Ordination   44

6   Walls of Jericho   57

7   Not Me But Us . . .   74

8   At the Edge   82

9   Reflections   90

APPENDIX 1   The Deaconess Order   99

APPENDIX 2   A Brief Historical Survey   106

APPENDIX 3   'Celebration for a Prioress'   111

Acknowledgements

Many people have contributed to the writing of this book as their lives have interacted with mine. I am grateful to them all for what they have been to me. My special thanks are due to family and friends, especially members of the Support Group, who, through their prayers, and in many practical ways, have helped me on my journey.

I wish to record particular thanks to Bishop John S. Spong for his warmth, support, encouragement and willingness to receive me into his diocese for the testing of my vocation. When he ordained me to the priesthood a year ago he broke a barrier, and I am glad that my previous English diocesan bishop, the Rt Revd Mervyn Stockwood, was also present to share in the act of ordination, thus linking the two Provinces of the Anglican Communion of which I am part.

I am grateful to Mrs Laura Hoskins who typed the manuscript of the book for me and to Fr Bede Thomas Mudge OHC and the Revd Alison Palmer who read the text and offered many helpful comments and suggestions.

Finally, I wish to thank the following people for extracts from letters and statements which appear in the book: The Rt Revd Ronald Bowlby, the Revd Alan Cotgrove SSJE, Deaconess Diana McClatchey, the Rt Revd Michael Marshall, the Revd Alison Palmer, the Rt Revd John Spong, and the Rt Revd Mervyn Stockwood.

December 1982
New York

Foreword

It is not my intention to offer a rationale for the ordination of women to the priesthood. Others have already done this convincingly. Rather I choose to share with my readers the personal struggle of one woman to realize that vocation. It has been a struggle characterized by joy and pain; hope and frustration; death and resurrection. I try to tell it with honesty, and this is no easy task, for it demands a degree of self-analysis and vulnerability, which is uncomfortable. But I believe it needs to be told, for endless abstractions about women and priesthood prevent encounter with persons, persons who cry out to be heard and understood. Until women are visibly part of the liturgical and sacramental life of the Church in England — and many parishioners have never even seen a deaconess leading worship — there will be debate based on fantasy, and an incomplete representation of God, who is neither male nor female.

I write to encourage my sisters in Christ who continue to wait, and pray, and work for the day when the Church of England is ready to test their vocations to this ministry. Some have hoped for many years that this time will come soon. I write to appeal to those who, in principle support the priesting of women, to engage with us in the task of achieving this end. I write to those who are uncertain, who are anxious about adjusting to change, to encourage them to face their fear with openness. And I write to those who are at present opposed to the ordination of women, for among them I count some of my close friends. I owe a good deal to several priests, and my previous suffragan bishop, with whom I have worked, prayed, and agonized over this issue. I respect their deeply held convictions and I am grateful for the understanding and affirmation I have received from them. Our conversations have compelled me to examine more critically my own position and have eradicated some of the caricatures and stereotypes of the Opposition. The often painful but honest sharing of differences has been creative and I believe the Church is big enough to contain us!

My ordination to the priesthood in the United States of America marks not so much an end of the Pilgrimage as a continuing with new vision. The human journey has many contours; the challenges and choices we face plunge us into conflict, and that is an inevitable and necessary part of our growth towards authenticity of being. As long as we live it will continue, and the response we make determines how far we move towards achieving the wholeness which is our destiny as women and men created in God's image. As a priest then, I continue that journey, still stumbling, still shocked by my own shallowness, still needing to commit myself daily to living the gospel of hope. And I find in penitence and joy the strength to reaffirm my 'Yes' to God, who is always dynamically involved in the 'stuff of life', and always urging me on, enabling me to make the simple yet profound prayer of Dag Hammarskjöld my own:

> For all that has been, thanks:
> To all that shall be, yes.

1 *Surprised by Joy*

During the winter of 1973 I discovered the joy of God and, like C. S. Lewis, I was surprised.[1] He was a reluctant convert to Christianity, while I cannot remember a time when I did not not believe, but mine had been a religion of duty to a deity who laid heavy obligations upon me. Fun was something which belonged to 'the world' and faith meant leaving earthly pleasures in order to pursue heavenly reward. It demanded effort and grim determination. For some thirty years I had lived with this understanding of Christianity. Now I discovered that God was joy, freedom, life.

The context of this discovery was a new and demanding job. For six years I taught religious education in British High schools, and then spent a year teaching and travelling in South Africa after completing studies for a theological degree. In September 1973 I returned to England to become Head of religious studies at a High school in a suburb of London, where racial conflict and social deprivation generated resentment towards authority figures. Truancy was at an all-time high, discipline in the classroom a continual struggle — many teachers had simply given up the effort to educate and had settled for containing the class during the thirty-five-minute period — and any sense of community was generally lacking. My task was to teach religious education in such a way that pupils could arrive at a set of values which would give meaning and purpose to life; and I felt impotent. Not only did the environment present overwhelming problems but, for me, religious practice had become a habit devoid of any sustaining power. I needed it as part of what I was as a human person, yet it gave no deep meaning or motivation to my work. How could I go on teaching that faith gives purpose to life, when it was giving little to mine?

For many years I had attended an Evangelical free church but often felt drawn to the liturgy and worship of the Church of

England. It was to the Anglican church that I now turned and, in the supportive environment of St Andrew's Church, Chorleywood, I was surprised by joy. The church was alive with expectancy and hope, consciously seeking renewal, and newcomers felt accepted no matter where they were on their Christian pilgrimage. I was drawn there by the vitality of the worship and experienced a revitalization of faith which enabled me to look on the world with new eyes. I discovered a fresh energy and confidence to teach and minister in the school, as well as a renewed sense of purpose and of the reality of God alive in the world. A few months later I was confirmed in St Alban's Abbey by the present Archbishop of Canterbury, who was then bishop of the diocese.

At the beginning of 1975 I moved to London to take up an appointment as lecturer in biblical studies at Wilson Carlile College. This too was a cause for joy since I wanted to use my theological training to help prepare others for ministry and here men and women were equipping themselves, as Church Army officers, for professional lay ministry in the Church of England. However as I began teaching in the college I found that my new openness to God and to life also led me inward. The mid-seventies represented a period of iconoclasm for me. One by one my idols were shattered, and I entered into that dark place where there is no certainty, and where only faith can sustain. But I went willingly. Somehow through all the groping, the enveloping blackness, I began to discover God and silence. I came to understand the risk of faith. The belief that God is and God loves grew, but the sense-experience of that reality was all too often lacking. Sometimes I seemed to be grasping the cliff edge with my fingernails, but it did not give way. The living Christ urges us into the future, to struggle, hope, doubt and believe without the illusion of absolute certitude. That was where I found myself and the structures, which had supported in the past, were gone.

As time went on I found I could no longer with integrity maintain the narrowly conservative stance which for many years had been my support. I continued to value the love for the Scriptures which I had learned, and to respect the concern for communicating the gospel which is characteristic of Evangelical Christianity, but the Catholic emphasis on the sacraments and an incarnational approach to theology expressed more fully the truth about God as I was beginning to understand it. I read many Catholic writers — my greatest discovery at this time was Thomas Merton — and I decided I needed time to think and pray, so spent a few days at an ecumenical retreat centre. Here Roman Catholic, Methodist, Orthodox and Anglican believers lived together in community and visitors were welcomed to share their life. One morning I went into the Blessed Sacrament chapel to pray. I knelt looking at the crucifix above the altar and then at the tabernacle, and felt overwhelmed by the presence of Christ in that place and in a special way in the sacrament. I was rather shocked by this. That which I had been taught emphatically to repudiate, and which made no sense to my intellect, now invaded my being as truth.

I had read and thought a good deal about the sacrament of reconciliation — a far happier term than penance — and was particularly impressed with the emphasis in the Roman Catholic Church since the second Vatican Council, on the healing power of confession and absolution, and the encouragement to move from the concept of the anonymous priest in a dark box to an informal, open sharing in prayer between priest and penitent. I had not at that time met any Anglican priest who felt secure enough to dispense with the traditional form of confession. No doubt the confessional has often been used as a means of keeping us like children, encouraging a dependence on the prohibitions and instructions of paternalistic priests. But to reject the sacrament, because it has been misunderstood and misused, is to impoverish and deprive Christian people of a means of spiritual growth and power. At this time it met a deep need for me, and I experienced a renewal of energy to go further into the 'dark wood', healed of some of the fearful resistance to uncertainty.

In addition to teaching biblical studies I was working on a Master of Theology degree in the area of New Testament. It was rumoured in Wilson Carlile College that I had been appointed to counterbalance the other biblical studies lecturer, who was an ardent Anglo-Catholic priest! Certainly the Evangelical students were ecstatic when they heard that the new lecturer had obtained a BD at the London Bible College, but their ecstasy was short lived. It was difficult for them to be attending lectures and seminars led by one who had moved on and it was disconcerting for me. I was searching for truth. They wanted uncertainty dispelled, and definite statements to reject or receive. For me it was an enriching journey of self-discovery. My New Testament professor at King's College was exceptionally patient as he read in my essays closely argued rejections of such themes as substitutionary atonement, and attempts to deal with Pauline passages which I considered anti-feminist. I learned that it was possible to allow each of the biblical writers to be rooted in his own context and social milieu without devaluing the biblical record. This more radical approach to Scripture was liberating and challenging and I believe it saved me from constructing out of High Church belief and practices, a new set of walls in which to hide. The parish of All Saints, Margaret Street, London had become my Mecca, as it continues to be for many commuters, who travel long distances to be present at the High Mass on Sunday mornings. I could only go occasionally because of commitments in my own parish but these were times of pure indulgence, when I could be passively enveloped in incense, glorious music and solemn liturgy.

Shortly after beginning work at the College I had been admitted and licensed as a Lay Reader. In England this meant that I was qualified to lead services, assist at Holy Communion and preach. I was surprised to discover when I moved to America that Lay Readers are often given little training and are literally readers of lessons who may also hold a Bishop's licence to administer the chalice. Very few have been trained to preach. I had to overcome initial anxiety that it was not appropriate for me, as a woman, to do these things but once I began to minister, grew more and more convinced of the rightness of it. More than that, I sensed that it was not enough. This is not to suggest that lay ministry is less valuable than the ordained ministry, only that I felt I was being called to something else. I began considering all sorts of possibilities, including the religious life, but somehow could not envisage myself as a nun, unless I joined one of the more radical Roman Catholic orders. And I was very definitely an Anglican. All the Anglican Sisters I had met at that time were from very traditional communities; they wore black habits and looked solemn, and, much as I appreciated retreats made in their houses, I could not imagine myself entering the life. Fortunately by this time I had found an Anglican priest to be my spiritual director, and I began exploring with him how I might respond to the growing sense of vocation to ministry.

One afternoon the Principal of the College had said to me as we drove to a meeting, 'You would make a good priest, Liz'. I had been surprised by the suddenness of the remark, coming to me in a dislocated moment, and had not seriously thought further about it. I had deep-seated prejudices against women. Even though I myself had begun to preach and lead public worship, I was not sure I liked other women doing these things! It was inconceivable that a woman could appropriately stand behind the altar and celebrate Holy Communion, yet if I were a man it is what I would have wanted to do. I was beginning to hear of groups pressing for the ordination of women to the priesthood, but was certainly not ready to give them my support. I was caught in a dilemma: God seemed to be urging me to deeper commitment, I sensed that it should be some lifelong form of offering, ideally I would like to be a priest, women could not be priests, how then could I fulfil my vocation?

I spent a lot of time thinking, agonizing and praying that summer and, after visiting various religious communities to discover more about their rules, and talking with the Dean of Women's Ministry in the Diocese of Southwark, decided reluctantly to seek ordination as a deaconess. My reluctance lay not in the lifelong commitment this involved, but in the fact that it is a confused order with a strange history,[2] which does not lead to priesthood in the Church of England, and I was now more than ever convinced that I should be a priest. However this was the one form of ordained ministry which was open to me and so, following the usual lengthy examination and selection process, I was approved for the Deaconess order.

At the end of September 1978 I arrived at our Diocesan Retreat and Conference Centre for the four days of preparation and pre-ordination retreat. Those four days turned out to be some of the most painful I have ever had to endure. The Retreat conductor, the Revd Richard Buck, prefaced his first address by apologising for his use of masculine language throughout the retreat, and explained that although the two women present would not be moving on to priesthood, we would be able to take much of what he had to say as appropriate to our own ministry. Each one of his addresses set before us a very high view of priesthood. We heard of the privilege, the awesome responsibility, the pain and the joy of this ministry. We learned that it meant servanthood not paternalism, that priests were to be visible signs in the community of the reconciling love of Christ, that to them was committed the inexpressible joy of pronouncing God's blessing and forgiveness, of celebrating the mystery of the Body and Blood of Christ. I found myself wanting to cry out, 'Yes, this *is* what it is all about, this *is* a model of priesthood I find credible, that I want to express'. And I knew none of it was for me. I experienced the deepest sense of deprivation I have ever known. Some of the men present would be made deacons kneeling beside me on Sunday, and a year later would be ordained priests. The rest were to be priested on this occasion. It was as though the church was slamming a monstrous iron door in my face, and I was left outside, cold and rejected.

On the evening before my ordination I met with Richard and he received the full force of my rage, bitterness, self-pity and despair. We had talked together earlier that year about the ordination of women, to which he was strongly opposed. I believe we listened to each other then, trying to understand and appreciate a view totally opposed to our own, yet to respect the integrity of each other. I wonder, in retrospect, how many men would have allowed themselves to be subjected for four days to the extolling of a ministry from which they were ultimately to be excluded. I believed it was important for Richard to understand the pain I was feeling, and after our conversation I made my confession. This was important, for though I appreciated his spirituality and much of what he had said, I hated him for the anguish his addresses had caused me and the insensitivity which enables men to go on subjecting women to this kind of humiliation. It truly was a sacrament of reconciliation.

Ordinations in Southwark Cathedral are highly organized and impeccably rehearsed. They take place twice yearly at Petertide and Michaelmas and it is only rarely that ordinations are held elsewhere in the diocese. The occasion of my ordination, 1st October 1978, was the first on which the new rite was used. The ordination of deacons took place first and the group of us knelt before the bishop and his two suffragans for the laying on of hands. 'Send down the Holy Spirit upon your servant Elizabeth for the office and work of a deacon in your Church.' I had made the same vows, taken the same oaths of obedience, received the same charge as the men and, kneeling with them, heard the same words spoken. The diocesan bishop, the Rt Revd Mervyn Stockwood, told me that in his eyes I was a deacon in the threefold order of ministry the 'Holy Orders' of the Church. Yet when I received my licence to officiate and other credentials, there was the word 'deaconess' according to the canons of the Church of England. My name appeared in the clergy lists in the diocesan directory, but in deanery and diocesan synods I must take my place in the House of Laity. It was customary in Southwark for deaconesses to wear stoles when assisting at the Eucharist, but this was questionable practice as far as the canons were concerned. However, at the final ordination service at which he presided before retiring, Bishop Stockwood made his view of women and the diaconate even more explicit by vesting the one woman being ordained with a stole.

It was with mixed feelings that I returned with family and friends to my flat to celebrate the occasion. I knew that within a few weeks the General Synod would vote on proposals to remove the legal barriers to the ordination of women to the priesthood, and, in spite of a systematic and highly organized campaign by opponents, those of us who waited for the Church to test our vocations hoped there might be a breakthrough. Yet I knew that I was going to have to live with tension whatever the outcome, for though the diaconate was a step towards my vocation, I would be suspended for years at least in this interim state, and I did not feel it was my ultimate goal. Moreover, I knew that the more articulate I became, the more of a threat I would pose to those who were not ready to consider that women might be priests. Although I did not know her at the time, I found the Revd Carter Heyward one of the first women ordained to the priesthood in America, had already expressed clearly that sense of threat when she wrote these words in her book *A Priest Forever*.

> In a society and a Church in which woman has been put into a place out of which she cannot move, any effort on her part to burst out of this place will be considered strange or abnormal. Those invested with institutional authority are likely to get their backs up and balk defensively at her efforts. For such a woman is a threat to both men and women who have heavy investment in maintaining the present order.
>
> And the threat is not imaginary. It is real. As women enter into new ecclesiastical roles, with responsibilities not only for decision-making and leadership in heretofore male arenas of activity, but also for new symbol-building, the present order will change. All roles, those of both men and women, will change.
>
> Our transforming power is not inherent to our gender, for we are simply human, like our brothers. Our power lies in our having been born, nurtured, and acculturated into a corporate symbol: a symbol not necessarily of 'feminity', but rather a symbol of difference. Together, we offer a difference to the Church, a difference that includes the corporate experience of exclusion, and the particular experiences of being daughter, wife, mother, lover, and the various other roles we have played.[3]

2 *Let the Women Keep Silence . . .*

All of us are shaped by our past. Our growth as Christians depends to some degree on our awareness of this conditioning and our willingness to change. Sometimes as we reflect on the events of our lives and the relationships which touched us deeply, we discern the movement of God in and through our experience. We are in the process of 'becoming' and all of our history has the potential to lead us into further self discovery as we reflect upon it.

I was born beneath the shadow of St Ethelreda's parish church in 'Old Hatfield', Hertfordshire, though the designation 'old' was appended only after the advent of the sprawling new town that devoured the woods and fields which were my childhood playground. The church stands at the top of a hill and our terraced house, with tiny backyard, could be reached by a steady climb past more illustrious dwellings in Church Street or by Jacob's Ladder. The latter consisted of stone steps ascending steeply from the lower road, a joy to me but a nightmare to my mother carrying shopping and managing a pushchair.

The first time I entered church, on the occasion of my baptism, I registered disapproval by screaming throughout the service. The vicar was unperturbed, assuring my distracted mother that I was driving out the devil, a claim she has had good reason to question many times since! As a toddler I loved to visit the Children's Corner with its strange pictures of Jesus in long skirts, and small paste pots filled with wild flowers. And I loved to play in the churchyard.

Sunday School took place on Saturday mornings! On one of the early occasions when I attended, Miss Scott asked if any of the children would like to sing a hymn or chorus. I instantly volunteered with, 'Gee-up, Neddy, to the Fair'. It was years before I understood why this caused mirth! Later my mother became the teacher and classes were held in our home. Three things are engraved on my mind from those occasions. First, there was the joy of preparing for other children to come; pencils to sharpen, pictures to hang from the knobs on the dresser (better known as the 'somewhere-to-put-it'), and clean sheets of paper set ready for drawing. Then there were the rolls of brightly-coloured modelling wax — not plasticine — slowly warming to malleability by the black kitchen range. And thirdly, there was the small boy who lost interest in drawing and instead sat sucking his pencil. It happened to be one of the indelible kind and we had to take him home and explain how he came by a purple mouth and tongue. We were afraid he might have poisoned himself!

When I was five my paternal grandfather died and we moved to the Gun Inn. My father now became proprietor of the pub maintaining a family tradition going back some eighty years. The house was built in the late eighteenth century and was originally a coaching inn used by travellers along the Great North Road. Little remained of the original building but the stables were still intact — these were rented out as garages when we moved in — and there was a skittle alley to play in. Here I organized my younger brother and sister into performing at concerts for an audience of friends and neighbours. The raised section, where the skittles would have been, made an ideal stage and my mother was coerced into parting with blankets to use as curtains.

There was one other shed occupied by 'Old Het'. He must have had another name but I never knew it. At one end was his bed covered with threadbare blankets, coats and sacks; in the middle an upright chair placed in front of the old-fashioned round stove on which he cooked (all the ingredients going into a single pot), and at the other end a big sideboard; food and his few other possessions were kept in this. He also had a cut-throat razor with a strop hanging just inside the door. We were forbidden to go inside 'Het's shed' and that made it a tantalizingly desirable place to us children. Sally, our mongrel bitch, had her puppies in there on a pile of sacks. Het used to kill our chickens when we needed one for dinner, and I remember watching one day with fascinated horror as he wrung a hen's neck and told me that chickens could still run round after they were dead! Eventually he grew too old to care for himself, had a slight stroke and went into an old age home after which he quickly died. The clinical efficiency and strangeness of his new way of life was too much for this independent, colourful old character, but we all missed him ambling up and down the yard.

I remember only two visits back to our parish church during these years at The Gun. A neighbour took my sister and me along one Sunday morning, for my father was occupied with 'opening time', and my mother with a new baby. During the service my sister dropped her prayer book and was scolded by the lady who took us. I was irate and changed places so that I sat between the guardian of the books and my sister to protect her. The second time I went I had a bad cough and the Rector, far less patient than the one who had baptized me amidst uproar, demanded that I be taken out. This action provoked such anger at home that it was decided we would not attend there again, though I did go to King's Messengers for a while. This was a kind of children's Bible Class sponsored by the parish church, and I was once a piece of chalk in a missionary play that they organized!

Our local Public Library was housed in two small rooms attached to the Congregational Church. We were avid readers, and I suppose it was through regular visits to the library that we became aware of the church and subsequently joined the Sunday School. It was there I learned that John 3.16 was 'the gospel in a nutshell', and was introduced to inter-church rallies. These were annual events where youngsters from all the Congregational churches in the district gathered to consume quantities of orange squash and to compete with one another in reciting biblical texts and poems. I joined rather late in the season so other children were well advanced in their memorizing of appropriate verses. I was assigned a poem beginning, 'Abou Ben Adam may his tribe increase', and instructed to learn it by the appointed day. When my turn to recite came I stood before the assembled company in some unfamiliar church, uttered the first few lines and lapsed into embarrassed silence. I think I was still awarded some kind of certificate for my efforts. Occasionally after Sunday School I would attend morning service with the couple who taught us. It was generally pretty dull, but I felt very grown up. The only thing I remember about sermons was one on the Trinity which, we were told, might be compared to a maple leaf.

On a week night there was a Bible Club which I also joined. This was called 'Seekers' or 'Searchers', I believe, and it involved a scheme of reading and learning lists of texts as well as games and singing. I was beginning to acquire a taste for religion and soon became a helper, sometimes even giving the 'talk' on these evenings. Later, I made friends with a girl from a Brethren family. Her father was an 'Elder' and I was rather frightened of him. She took me to a rally in St Albans, organized by the Junior Young Life Campaign, an evangelistic organization primarily committed to 'winning souls for Christ.' It was at this meeting that I first became aware of the Evangelical emphasis upon personal conversion and, in later years, when called upon to declare when and where I was 'saved' I generally referred back to this meeting.

For the next four years I went to the Sunday Bible Class and evening meeting at the local Brethren Assembly. We would gather on Sunday afternoons, first to sing CSSM choruses and then divide into groups for teaching. There was no permanent Hall so the Assembly rented an old cottage. There were only three of us old enough to be in the Bible Class so we mounted the rickety wooden stairs to an upstairs room where my friend's mother taught us. I cannot now remember anything of what we learned, but I got to know the patterns on the wallpaper well, and recall the irritation I felt if she talked too long, since my favourite pop singer was on the radio a few minutes after we were due to end. My mother, brother, and sister came along to the Gospel Meeting with me on Sunday evenings. We sang lustily from *Redemption Hymnal* about being 'washed in the blood of the Lamb', 'marching to Zion', and 'bringing in the sheaves'. Solemn-looking men came from other Assemblies to address us at length, usually on some obscure Old Testament passage. There was a small harmonium, which had to be pedalled furiously, to accompany the singing.

I now began to understand that it was not only necessary to be saved but also to be baptized by immersion as a 'witness' to that experience. Of course, there was no baptistry at the cottage, so when candidates were forthcoming members would travel to a nearby hall for the event. Before being baptized it was necessary to 'give a testimony' and that was an added attraction at the evening Gospel Service prior to the baptism. It posed a problem, however, because St Paul said women must not speak in church, yet female candidates had to declare their faith. It was decided that, since he had said nothing about them singing publicly, it would not be an infringement of scriptural principles if they chose a favourite hymn and sang it as their testimony! Whether the woman was musically gifted or tone deaf was immaterial.

During these years there were other evangelistic events which I attended. At a rally led by evangelist Tom Rees in the Royal Albert Hall, an appeal was made for people in the audience to go forward if they wanted to be saved. My friend's mother — who had probably observed me gazing vacantly at the wallpaper during her lessons — asked me if I would like to go, assuring me they would all wait. I declined, much to her disappointment, but often wondered, as the pressure to conform built up, whether it would not have been better to respond and get this 'going forward' requirement over with.

Soon we began hearing of a famous American evangelist who was coming to London for mass meetings, and arrangements were made to transport coach parties to Harringay Arena. I went to one of these meetings, and once again felt uncomfortable as the organ played and the choir sang 'Just as I am without one plea', while Billy Graham urged us again and again to go forward where we would find counsellors ready to lead us to Christ.

That year I went with a friend to a holiday conference held in a school on the south coast under the auspices of the National Young Life Campaign. The importance of Bible reading and prayer were daily urged upon us, and we met each morning and evening for teaching and worship. The Bible was interpreted literally, and I found this conservative approach to Scripture and the emphasis on personal salvation appealing. I was beginning to be intoxicated with the kind of Evangelical religion which made authoritative assertions and clear imperatives. It offered a security at a time when I was dealing with the uncertainties of adolescence and needing to find a personal identity.

I recall the next few years as a period of disorientation, anxiety and depression during which I engaged in an endless battle of wills with my father. He was a staunch Anglican, though not a churchgoer, and was utterly opposed to the Gospel Hall type of religion which I had adopted and into which I drew the rest of the family. My devotion to reading the Bible he dubbed religious mania, and the request to be baptized by immersion was met with enraged refusal.

The Brethren meetings gradually began to lose some of their appeal, since there were few other teenagers attending and no kind of activity in which we could be involved. Even then I had a sense of wanting to lead and teach others but I was neither male nor properly baptized so this was not an option. Then I met an old school friend who had been converted at a Billy Graham rally and who invited me to the church she was attending six miles away. We went together the next Sunday evening and it appeared to be exactly what I was looking for. A crowded Evangelical free church mainly filled with young people, enthusiastic singing, and good Bible-based preaching. There was a lively Youth Club on Friday nights and an enthusiastic young pastor. I was soon attending the services regularly, teaching a Sunday School class, and going to Friday Fellowship meetings as well as the midweek Bible Study and Prayer meeting.

Soon after I began attending this church we began a series of Bible studies in the Pastoral epistles, a series which lasted some two years. We were taught that these writings provided the blueprint for church government: autonomous local congregations with several bishops, or elders, and deacons, all of whom were to be tested in the prescribed manner. The most serious attention was to be given to sound doctrine, those who did not subscribe to it were to be excluded and strict church discipline maintained. We all felt we were on the verge of something new and exciting for we had discovered what lost and erring Christendom had ceased to practise. We had found the truth, though as I was to discover painfully years later, it was not the truth which set people free. We heard a great deal about the Reformers and were urged to return to their teaching (even other evangelicals were not necessarily considered 'sound'). So I read the Reformers, attended Puritan Conferences, and became thoroughly committed to John Calvin's theology! That other patterns of Church order were reflected in the New Testament, that the Pastorals might be late, non-Pauline and emerging from one small section of the Christian church, or that centuries of history might have something to contribute to the discussion on church government and ministry, were not even considered. A fundamentalist approach to the Bible precluded such questions and even where Paul seemed to be arguing against Paul, texts were somehow manipulated so that he agreed with himself. In fact, even James and Paul were shown to be the best of friends over matters of faith and works by this method. I was thoroughly convinced that the Scriptures taught that I, as a woman, might not teach, preach or lead public worship (though I might pray aloud extemporarily at the prayer meeting). I found this difficult, but knew I could not question God who had decreed for all time the subordination of women. However, I was appointed a 'lady deacon', a mark of high honour and an indication of my doctrinal soundness.

When I announced that I was going to train as a teacher of religious education, it caused some alarm in the church and I was warned of the dangers of 'modernism' and 'higher criticism'. However, I managed to hold fast to my Evangelicism during the years of training and played a leading role in the College Christian Union. On the completion of my course, I taught in schools within easy reach of the church, finally as Head of the Religious

Education Department of a Comprehensive School. During this time, all sorts of questions were beginning to form themselves in my mind. Was it reasonable to suppose that the version of Christian truth we held was the only or whole truth, and did we have the right and obligation to impose that on those who were without it? Were they really lost if they interpreted the gospel differently? Was it in the spirit of Christ that we demanded conformity at every point to a doctrinal system, and excluded from the fellowship those who did not possess our certainty? Why were questions so ruthlessly suppressed, especially when these related to biblical interpretation? There was certainly a great deal of Bible study taking place, but serious biblical scholarship was scorned and the conclusions of most current theologians rejected. The Bible contained 'unchanging truth'; the Reformers had grasped it, and we must go on proclaiming yesterday's certainty.

At the time I accepted all this fully, even though questions and doubts would not go away. Now I would suggest that when orthodoxy is allowed to eclipse love and respect, the gospel is no longer being proclaimed. Jesus was constantly the target of attack by the religious guardians of the faith in his day. He was a friend to the doubters, outcasts, and marginalized people whom he met. When they encountered him he affirmed them as men and women of value, kindling in them a longing for the wholeness he embodied. Religious officialdom could not tolerate such acceptance of the despised, for its members depended on their superior knowledge of truth, their righteousness, for any sense of personal value. The only way to deal with deviants like Jesus was to discredit his message and suggest the existence of a sinister plot to lead the multitude into error. A similar discrediting of other Christian churches was commonplace in our fellowship. Even other Evangelical groups were not necessarily sound. We received several visits from a 'converted' American Roman Catholic priest whose mission was to enlighten us about the evils of Romanism. He dredged up obscure examples of religious ceremonial and canon law which were clearly unscriptural, even pagan in origin. Even in those pre-Vatican II days many contemporary Roman

Catholics would have been amazed to learn that this was what they believed!

This kind of religion instills fear, especially the fear of independent thought and of being wrong. Yet I was stifled by it, and my integrity was at risk as long as I refused to face the growing disquiet within. I was longing to break free, my love of theology was growing and I began to explore the idea of further study. I thought that the London Bible College, an interdenominational institution with high academic standards, was the kind of environment I needed so I applied for entry. I was accepted for Courses leading to the University of London external BD degree. More warnings followed. In spite of its Evangelical foundation, the college was not unequivocally 'Reformed' and even here I might be led astray!

In many ways, the two years at LBC were enriching. I made new friends from a variety of churches and backgrounds, found the stimulation of academic study rewarding, and especially enjoyed worshipping regularly at an Anglican church. Throughout the years of non-conformist worship, I had loved the liturgy and appreciated the dignity of services in the Church of England whenever I attended.

There were frustrations about study at LBC however. Because the college has a clear Evangelical doctrinal basis, its faculty is committed to maintaining this approach to Scripture and theology. Not all students read for public examinations, but those who do find themselves having to study texts and ideas at variance with the college's position. This problem is dealt with by the teaching staff elucidating the material to be studied and then trying to offer answers or approaches. There seemed to be little place for uncertainty or variety of interpretation. I was finding some of the set texts extremely exciting and the answers unsatisfactory. In particular, I found myself often in accord with the more Catholic writers. I began to experience a tension between what long conditioning and the college taught, and new insights which 'rang true' for me.

I received my degree and left England for a year in South

Africa, where I taught school and travelled. I worked in High Schools for the privileged white pupils of Port Elizabeth and soon adjusted to a very good standard of living, a high salary and black servants. True, I felt uncomfortable when black people moved aside to let me pass in the streets or be served first in shops, and when they were left behind in the queue despite seats being available in the 'white's only' section of the bus. I was shocked when I entered a black township, even though I was on an officially organized tour and we were not shown the worst hovels. When I hear South Africans attempting to justify the inhumanity of government policy there (offering the euphemism 'separate development' for apartheid), I am aware of how imperceptibly a patronizing attempt to 'understand the blacks' or offer minor improvements in their lot has an anaesthetic effect on the conscience. I could not justify remaining there in my privileged position, though the full impact of the experience came later, when *I* felt marginalized by the Church because of my sex and suddenly saw many parallels.

Both in South Africa, and previously in England, I had taught in good schools set in middle-class areas. The doubts and questions raised through my earlier religious experience and study for a theological degree had been largely shelved during the year overseas. Some were intellectual questions about approaches to theology, others related to the relevance of faith, of *my* faith, in the present. When I returned to England in 1973, they could be avoided no longer. My new job demanded honesty; children in the school where I now taught were quick to detect insincerity. 'How can I believe in a God of love when my father is in gaol and beats us each time he gets out?' 'How can religion help me find a job when I leave school?' 'Why does my mother leave us kids home each night while she's at the pub?' 'Can God help my sister who is fourteen and pregnant?' All this precipitated a crisis of faith: a crisis which led to the discovery of joy described in the last chapter.

As I reflect on the years leading to this event I believe the vocation to priesthood was contained embryonically within them.

18

However, I was unable to recognise it. To compensate for the turmoil of adolescence, I adopted a belief system which provided security by its dogmatic assertions, one of which focused on the subordinate role of women. Thus I was compelled to suppress any desire for leadership in the Church, and to deny a part of myself without which I felt incomplete. I did not break free from this stance even during study for a theological degree in spite of the inner urgings to do so. When I did finally arrive at the point where I could allow my sense of vocation to become conscious — and by then I was an Anglican — I found that the Church did not want what I had to offer, and taught me to believe that her rejection of my gifts was divinely inspired. Florence Nightingale's lament still rings true even though the Church has opened the door a crack to allow women to become parish workers and deaconesses:

> I would give her [the Church] my head, my hand, my heart. She would not have them. She did not know what to do with them. She told me to go back and crochet in my mother's drawing room. 'You may go to the Sunday School if you like', she said. But she gave me no training even for that. She gave me neither work to do for her, nor education to do it.

3 *The Ministry of Reconciliation*

On 8 November, little more than a month after I was ordained to the diaconate, the General Synod of the Church of England debated a proposal to prepare legislation which would remove the barriers to the ordination of women to the priesthood. I remember well the day on which the vote was taken. I was not present but all day I thought of, and inwardly agonized with, my sisters in Christ who sat silent as the Debate continued. Some of them had waited and worked for many years to realize their vocations. I had hoped for a comparatively short time that the Church would soon be ready to test my vocation to the priesthood. But it was not to be.

That evening as I walked into our college chapel for the Eucharist, one of the students who had been seated in the Visitors' Gallery at Church House waited to greet me. Her face told me that the answer had been 'No'. Somehow I managed to sit through the service, trying to draw strength from Christ the Servant of Yahweh, despised and rejected of men. Those words took on new depth and poignancy.

> He was despised and rejected by men . . . he was despised and we esteemed him not . . . he was oppressed, and he was afflicted, yet he opened not his mouth . . . by oppression and judgement he was taken away.

I was unconsciously inserting the feminine pronoun! Afterwards I was surprised at the intensity of my feeling. I knew I looked devastated as we all left the chapel. The Principal, who was supportive of me personally and of the priesting of women in general, said, 'But you didn't really expect a "Yes" vote, did you?' I found it quite impossible to communicate an answer. What had I expected? My colleague, who shared the biblical studies teaching with me, was relieved by the negative vote, and could find no way to empathize with my feelings. I found his attitude totally paradoxical; in his approach to theology he was far more radical than I was, but when it came to ecclesiastical practice he retreated to a very traditional High Church position. I went home experiencing a profound sense of loneliness and isolation.

That night I had a dream. I was walking across a kind of rickety bridge constructed over a deep gorge, through which dark waters were rushing. To my left I saw a tree growing, profusely covered with leaves and ripe, golden grapefruit. Then I was standing on the top rung of a stepladder, precariously balanced on the wooden struts of the bridge. I was stretching for the largest, most luscious fruit at the top of the tree but it was hopelessly out of reach, the steps began to sway and I was in serious danger of plunging into the black, swirling waters below. I woke before I fell, but in the days and months that followed I struggled often in those deep waters sometimes overwhelmed by them. I learned to love the Psalms and through them to express my own pain and sense of rejection. The extremes of human experience are encapsulated in these expressions of ecstasy and despair which so enrich our liturgy, and I find myself in the company of the succession of God's people expressing devotion and rage.

> Out of the depths I cry to thee, O Lord!
> Lord, hear my voice.
> Ps. 130.1—2

> My soul is cast down within me, therefore I remember thee from the land of Jordan and of Hermon. Deep calls to deep at the thunder of thy cataracts; All thy waves and thy billows have gone over me.
> Ps. 42.6—7

> My God, my God, why has thou forsaken me?
> Ps. 22.1

The idea of grasping for the priesthood (which the dream seems to suggest), leaves me feeling uncomfortable. The inner workings of our psyche, which often become clear if we pay attention to dreams, do reveal aspects of ourselves we would rather disown. However, when we decide to allow them to challenge us they can become important points of growth. The dream proved to have a somewhat prophetic element. As long as I went on pushing at the barriers of the Church I might expect to be dislodged, or to be precariously balanced between hope and despair.

The joy of God did not evaporate over the next few months, but I am aware as I recall this period, that there was much negativity about it. The temptation to self-pity was ever present; objectivity about the Church of England became increasingly difficult, and it was easy to respond to rejection by hostility. If the next few pages seem defensive and gloomy it is probably because that was how I felt much of the time. In fact, I experienced a sense of being oppressed though I would not have then defined it in those terms.

A very positive event of 1978 was my appointment as a non-stipendiary member of staff at St Luke's with Holy Trinity, Charlton in South-east London. I owe the Rector, Tony Crowe, a great deal for the support he has given me, and I deeply respect his integrity. At times this has led him to support unpopular causes and to be the target of vicious attack. Few women in the Church of England have been offered the range of opportunities for ministry and liturgical function which I received at St Luke's. It is an eclectic parish, in which radical thinkers are at home, but which also embraces those of both Evangelical and Anglo-Catholic persuasion.

Much as I love good Anglo-Catholic worship, I have found it increasingly difficult to be present at services which are entirely male dominated. At St Luke's, women played as full a part as possible within the Church of England. The verger and senior church warden were women, and women shared equally with men as sidespersons, servers, acolytes, crucifers. I always stood with Tony behind the altar as he celebrated and, having led the Ministry of the Word, distributed Communion in both kinds. When we had a High Mass or celebrated the complex Easter Liturgy, I served as deacon. I well remember the first occasion on which I had to cense the Gospel before reading it. I had recently acquired contact lenses and was still adjusting to them. As I swung the censor, I found myself enveloped in clouds of smoke, and a thick fog clouded my vision making it almost impossible to read the opening words of the gospel.

These years then, represented a time of struggle and joy, of frustration and fulfilment. Some of my South African experience became alive to me, for often I felt marginalized and second class. But it was not all grim; there were times when I could laugh at myself, at the dear Old Church of England lumbering slowly into the twentieth century, at the antics of those who opposed change. Doris Lessing has some poignant comments on this essential sense of satirical fun on the part of the oppressed:

> There are other things in living beside injustice, even for the victims of it. I know an African short story writer whose gift is for satirical comedy, and he says that he has to remind himself, when he sits down to write, that 'as a human being he has the right to laugh'. Not only have white sympathisers criticised him for making comedy out of oppression, his compatriots do too. Yet I am sure that one day out of Africa will come a great comic novel to make the angels laugh, pressed as miraculously from the bitter savageries of the atrophy as was *Dead Souls.*[1]

A sense of fun, the ability to laugh at ourselves and our oppressors, above all, a deep sense of the joy of God are essential if we are to live hopefully and creatively through the pain.

When St Paul wrote, 'Christ reconciled us to God and gave us the ministry of reconciliation' (2 Cor. 5.18) he was expressing the heart of the Christian gospel. The purpose of reconciliation is to bring humankind into a relationship of peace with God, and that involves the ending of hostility and includes the reconciling of different factions between us. We western Christians 2,000 years on, have little comprehension of the magnitude of the claim that, in Christ, Jew and Gentile are reconciled and brought together to God (Eph. 2.14). The difficulty experienced by the early Church in adjusting to the full acceptance of non-Jewish believers, provides the closest biblical parallel to our problems today over women priests. I began to feel that the most creative way of

23

dealing with my disappointment was to try and act as an agent of reconciliation, entering into dialogue and listening to those who opposed the priesting of women.

Following the 1978 General Synod vote which rejected women priests, I found myself constantly thinking around the theme of reconciliation especially when I spent a few days in retreat with the Sisters of the Church at Ham Common. While I was there, Sister Joy gave me Andrew Elphinstone's book, *Freedom, Suffering and Love* to read and this helped me to make sense of some of the experiences of those days and also to formulate a direction for my own pilgrimage. First, I needed to be able to forgive those who said 'No' to women priests, to my vocation. Elphinstone writes:

> Forgiveness brings us face to face with pain, for, whatever else it is made up of, it is centrally the matter of dealing with pain: if you have not been hurt there is nothing to forgive. That is why it is the most exacting exercise of love . . . Pain is indeed the single most significant experience of humanity.
>
> It need not, however, be destructive or divisive; it need not proliferate or form vicious circles. What Christ was doing, in innermost meaning, in the crucifixion was to accomplish the dealing with pain in such a way that it could not be any of these things. In him love rose to its climax in meeting pain and injustice, to its most totally exacting dimension and remained unbroken. That is forgiveness, because whom you go on loving you do not any more even desire to condemn or revenge yourself upon. So man's forgiveness was assured but, almost as vital, the trail of man's forgiveness of man was blazed. The evil of man's proliferating estrangements was shown to be terminable.[2]

Consciously over those days I prayed for individuals through whom I had personally felt rejected as a woman with a vocation to priesthood; and that meant confronting my own hatred, anger, and desire for revenge. I tried to grasp the pain, to visualize those people as loved by God, and created in God's image; and I tried to love them in their sin and brokenness just as I knew myself thus loved and accepted by the Lord. It takes the confronting and experiencing of pain to accomplish its healing, but when we honestly face our own bitterness, self-pity, and fear then our struggle becomes creative and we enter more fully into the reality of the cross. I was finally able to reaffirm my own 'Yes' to God, and to respond positively to the ministry which was available to me at that time. At the end of the Retreat I wrote these words:

> I hear you, Lord
> Across the echoes of a million voices
> A clear, incisive word
> 'Follow me'.
> I hunger, Lord
> And find you set before me bruised and broken
> In suffering mankind
> 'Feed on me'.

On 17 November, 1978, the *Church Times* published a letter I wrote appealing for a greater tolerance among the disparate groups and calling on protagonists to 'hear' one another.

Sir, The Bishop of Truro rightly pointed out at the conclusion of the debate on the ordination of women to the priesthood that whichever way the vote went, there would be pain. I have found it distressing to witness over the last few months a hardening of attitudes on both sides, as well as acrimonious slanging matches and threats.

Like many others I prayed for the guidance of the Holy Spirit in this debate, and must accept that God honoured that prayer. But I do feel very deep pain, and I wonder whether any of those who find themselves committed to oppose moves to ordain women are willing to share it.

It seems to me that the gospel of reconciliation which we offer to the world has something important to say to us here. Can we begin to meet, share and pray together, to face honestly our differences in a spirit of love and tolerance?

Some of the most hopeful and creative conversations I have had recently have been with priests whose views on this issue are totally opposed to mine. I have received from them acceptance, respect and loving pastoral concern and I believe there has been mutual enrichment.

I would be glad to hear from any who are willing to explore further the possibility of such meeting and discussion without the desire to form yet another defensive, esoteric group.

In response to this letter I received several replies from lay people, most of them in favour of women priests, applauding my sentiments and offering to join any group to further mutual respect and understanding. After two weeks a priest from the Episcopal Church of Scotland wrote to tell me he remained utterly opposed to women priests but found, as he knelt before the altar to give thanks for the Synod vote, he was overcome by emotion and wept for the hurt, disappointed women, whom he visualized. Later, another priest from Devon wrote very honestly about his reasons for opposing the priesting of women and we corresponded several times. I received no reply from the Bishop of Truro to whom I wrote enclosing a copy of my letter, but the Rt Revd Michael Marshall, responded with sympathy and a promise to do all he could to affirm women's ministry.

At a meeting of women workers and deaconesses which took place shortly afterwards, I again raised the question of initiating dialogue between the opponents and supporters of women priests. The diocesan bishop was present, and the precentor of the cathedral offered the facilities of the cathedral for such a gathering. A small committee, chaired by the Bishop of Kingston, began to meet and plan for an evening conference which would: (a) inform people what women were already doing in the Church; (b) explore ways in which their ministry could be extended. We met in May 1979 and speakers included Roman Catholics and Anglicans, lay women, religious, and priests. My most vivid memory is of Mgr Bruce Kent's words spoken with some frustration, because the question of women priests had been carefully avoided all evening: 'Stop looking over your shoulders to see what Rome will think. You Anglicans have not shown a great deal of sensitivity to us in the past, why start now? If something is right, it is right, so get on with it and we'll get there eventually'.

Dealing with feelings of anger and despair did not end at Ham

26

Common, for I went on encountering chauvinism and rejection from those who found themselves unable to divorce their opposition to women priests from my valid ministry as a deaconess. The Church Army Training College undertook a Mission in Northampton during Easter 1978. The Church Army Officer who was leading my team had asked me to preach on our first Sunday, but when we arrived, the vicar greeted me with some disapproval and the words, 'So you're going to hold forth on Sunday morning?' His hostility was obvious, but I hoped that during a week of Mission the fact that I was a woman might become less important as we ministered together. It was a difficult time; clearly, one of my students, a male, was far more acceptable than I was. A year later when we were about to make a return visit, I called the vicar to confirm our travel arrangements and the schedule for the day. The leader of the team wanted to preach at the final evening service and had again asked me to preach in the morning. There was a silence when I passed on this information, and then the vicar said he really did not want me to preach at the morning Eucharist as the Bishop had said no lay person should do so; perhaps Captain would give the address instead! Since our previous visit I had been ordained; the Church Army Officer was clearly a layman, so it became evident that sexist prejudice had conditioned the response. After a night of agonizing over my own resentment, I decided that I would not go, for I believed that the vicar needed to confront his own prejudice; so I wrote explaining that I experienced his attitude as a rejection of a ministry endorsed by the Church and shared in his congregation, and asked him to use his discretion in explaining my absence. I never received a reply, and he avoided offering any explanation to his people.

Another time I was due to preach during a Church Army weekend in Bournemouth both at St Mary's and the daughter church. The solemn Evensong at St Mary's was a joy; I was welcomed warmly by the Rector, and thoroughly enjoyed the music, incense and dignity of the service; (I am sure my love of incense in worship springs not only from the aesthetic pleasure it brings, but from the delight in enjoying something forbidden and designated 'papist' in my youth!). The Eucharist that morning at the daughter church had been a very different experience. I had stayed overnight with the priest-in-charge and his wife, and it was clear that he was uncomfortable with me. Before the service I was asked if I would like breakfast and realized after I had been given a slice of toast to eat alone in my room that this constituted my first error. Of course, I should have fasted! When we got to the church, the priest sat me in front of the sanctuary next to the choir stalls while he got on with preparing for the service. I was ignored for about twenty minutes and he finally asked me if I wanted to join the procession. Since I had been sitting holding my robes as the church filled with worshippers, I said that I would prefer to go to the Vestry to put them on and then come in with everyone else. It had never been done before, a woman setting foot in the clergy vestry, but with difficulty he accepted the inevitable. If I had not asked the assisting priest at what point I should enter the pulpit I would never have known and would, in fact, have been 'boxed in' to my seat by the gospel procession. At the end of the service the procession went out by a different route which did not pass near my seat and I was left behind. I expected that the priest would at least collect me and take me to the back of the church to greet people when he returned, but he walked past, ignoring me to take up his position at the door.

I could go on multiplying instances of clerical insensitivity to female colleagues. Letters from a borough dean beginning, 'Dear Brothers'; not being invited to diocesan social functions (though wives of male clergy were included); a sudden request not to wear a stole because, although it is the usual practice in the diocese, such and such a Bishop will be present and might be upset. And all the time we wrestle with our need to protest (in which case we will be perceived as aggressive or petty) and our conditioning which tells us we should be compliant, undemanding and 'feminine'.

A year after my ordination the colleague, who had come as a layman to work with me teaching biblical studies, was ordained deacon. It was painful being present, for the men who entered the diaconate alongside me were priested at the same service. Of course, I rejoiced with Martin but felt my own sense of rejection more acutely. Next Michaelmas he was priested and this time the Southwark Branch of the Movement for the Ordination of Women were present to protest silently at the exclusion of women from the priesthood. We held an all night prayer vigil in the cathedral and in the morning members stood outside as guests arrived, handing out leaflets explaining our presence and giving a Michaelmas daisy to anyone who would accept it. Most of the ordinands received a daisy and the diocesan bishop wore one in his pectoral cross.

Four of us were inside the cathedral kneeling in silent prayer throughout the service, a priest from the diocese, an Anglican sister, and two deaconesses. For me the most liberating aspect of this rather difficult experience was the fact that we did not ask for a place to pray; we made a claim for ourselves by writing to the Provost saying we would be there. It is certainly true to say that the staff at Southwark were much more sympathetic than in many other dioceses; nevertheless, anxiety is generated if there is a hint that something untoward might happen to spoil the flow or procession of the service. For once we had not given total authority to those in power, we had risked being perceived as belligerent, or difficult, for we refused to live up to people's expectations of what women in the Church should be like. This is how we become more fully ourselves, more whole; and it is a battle all the way, because the spectres of fear created by our conditioning are ever ready to haunt us into inaction. Again, Carter has put this well:

> The most insidious demon against which we women have to contend is the human inclination to swallow and digest what is said about us.
>
> We begin to reclaim our souls when we are able to cast out this demon of self-doubt and move on — angrily, caringly, emphatically — in a knowledge that we have been violated not because we are 'confused,' 'aggressive,' 'sick,' or 'incompetent,' but rather because we are people who are attempting to live fully our potential.[3]

4 *Kaleidoscope*

Sometimes pattern and symmetry can be discerned through the chaotic jumble of events and ideas which make up our lives. But often we are temporarily paralyzed by some overwhelming pain or loss which absorbs our whole attention and distorts the picture. The kaleidoscope I possessed as a child was a source of fascination until I took it apart to find out how it worked and was left holding a few fragments of coloured glass. It has become an important symbol to me as I consider my 'Pilgrimage'.

The way we handle the broken pieces, our attitude to conflict and pain will determine whether or not we grow towards the wholeness God wills for us. Conflict can be destructive, but it can also be transfigured into a creative source of life and energy.

There is a terrible delusion under which many Christians labour — and with which some preachers collude — that faith in Christ transports you onto a new level of existence. Christ is presented as the solver of problems, the bringer of peace, acting in a magician-like manner to remove pain, fear and anxiety. But this neglects the truth that at the centre of Christian faith is the cross, the ultimate symbol of contradiction and conflict and any attempt to escape its implications indicates a choice of illusion instead of reality.

Sometimes as we look back over our lives we can see a pattern emerging. Mostly, though, we are aware of the disparate elements, the lack of cohesion and togetherness, broken fragments of glass. Much of the time our attention is concentrated on a single fragment, and being human means facing conflict, living with the fragmentary nature of life as, by faith, we journey towards that greater wholeness which it is our destiny to inherit in Christ. As I look back over the last few years, I glimpse design, and I recognize that the painful fragments are an essential part of it.

Late in 1979 I began to consider visiting America in order to meet with women priests, experience their ministry, and confront my own prejudice. Although I felt sure God was calling me to priesthood I still had some reservations about other women in that role. The appropriate way to deal with this kind of conditioned fear is not evasion but an honest facing of the feelings, and it seemed I could only do that by visiting one of the Provinces of the Anglican Communion where women priests were already a reality. Through a friend I contacted the Revd Alison Palmer in Washington, DC and she offered to set up meetings with women clergy during the summer of 1980 when I would be on holiday. I also decided to explore the possibility of finding work in the USA and of asking the Anglican church there to test my vocation to the priesthood.

Alison and I exchanged a series of letters in which she advised me of the canonical requirements and suggested ways of approaching bishops, and clergy deployment offices. She also pointed out that I would need the written support of my English bishop, and as much documentation as possible relating to my academic and pastoral training, in order to be considered by an American diocese. I began to feel reticent about the whole proposal. It seemed a formidable task. I was considering uprooting myself from home, leaving those still engaged in the struggle for women priests, making my vocation the primary goal. Was this selfish? I was concerned not to act in isolation from women in England and shared with as many as possible the course I was considering. I also shared my doubts with Alison. I received a firm reply in response to my diffidence:

> You said that you did not want to take off for the US for 'personal fulfilment'. I feel very strongly that you should not think of your plans in that way; no one accuses a man of seeking 'personal fulfilment' if he responds to a vocation to the priesthood, and I do not think you should allow anyone to make you feel guilty or selfish if you also respond to vocation by seeking ordination. Sometimes people will say to women that they should not worry about status or power but just humbly and quietly serve the Lord; my answer is that the same remark can be made to a man with a

31

vocation, but somehow it never seems to be. Furthermore, how can we serve the Lord *as priests* if the Church does not give us the power and status of priests so we can minister as priests?

I learned from this letter and my subsequent meetings with women priests in the States, that they usually had a far greater confidence in themselves and their call than most of us seeking priesthood in England.

On 27 June, 1980, I left London on a Laker flight to JFK airport, New York. The journey from the airport into the city was a nightmare — exchanging currency, finding a bus, carrying heavy luggage onto the subway and finally arriving at 42nd Street and 6th Avenue late in the evening. I felt lost and very alone, surrounded by the noise of the city I now love. It was a baptism of fire and I began to doubt the wisdom of coming at all. It was an enormous relief to find the Revd George Swanson parked across the street. I spent the first weekend in New Jersey. The Revd Katrina Swanson and George are both Episcopal priests who serve as rectors of adjoining parishes. On the Sunday morning I preached and served as deacon in Katrina's parish, (St John's, Union City). This was only the second time I had been present at a service in which the celebrant was a woman, (the first occasion had been a few weeks earlier when the Revd Carol Anderson had celebrated in St Paul's Cathedral Deanery for the Metropolitan Committee of MOW). On both occasions I found that, after initial thanksgiving for the joy of being present, I became unconscious of the gender of the celebrant. It seemed perfectly natural that the sacrament was presided over by a woman.

That same evening the ordination to the priesthood of the Revd Phyllis Edwards took place at St John's. Phyllis knew of my own sense of vocation to the priesthood, and from her experience of waiting many years to be ordained, was aware of the pain I felt over the Church of England's decision, 'not yet'. To show her solidarity with me she asked the bishop if I could function as the deacon at her ordination. Bishop John Spong (of Newark) agreed and expressed his regret that the Mother church was not yet ready to act on her own resolution that 'there are no fundamental theological objections to the ordination of women to priesthood'. The service was a mixture of tears and laughter, solemnity and joy. The Peace lasted for some fifteen minutes! Phyllis con-celebrated with the Bishop, who then received the sacrament from her. As far as I know this was the first time that a woman rector of a parish had presented a woman deacon for ordination to the priesthood.

During the reception after the service I spoke with Bishop Spong about the possibility of transferring to the American Episcopal Church in order to fulfil my vocation. He was cautious but optimistic and said he wanted an opportunity to discuss the implications of such a course of action with his brother bishops before proceeding. The next House of Bishops meeting was scheduled for late September so clearly no further action was possible until then.

The next four weeks were incredibly busy. I travelled up and down the East coast visiting women clergy, seminaries and diocesan offices. I celebrated Independence Day in Washington, DC, at the magnificent firework display, did some sightseeing there, and was present in the State Department when Richard Queen, one of the Iranian hostages arrived home. I also discovered Howard Johnson's ice cream! At the end of it all I felt exhilarated and exhausted. I returned to England with a notebook full of addresses, information, and advice about the way to proceed.

It was very clear that it would be difficult to transfer to the Episcopal Church in the USA without the support and com-mendation of my diocesan bishop in England. Just after I returned to London I went to see the Bishop of Southwark, the Rt Revd Mervyn Stockwood, to tell him of my discussions with Bishop Spong and to ask whether he would support me in a move to ECUSA. He had for many years declared himself in favour of the ordination of women, though he did not seem to be involved actively in any attempt to bring this about. He had always given the impression that he was rather uncomfortable in the company of women, and the deaconesses and women workers of the diocese tended to feel overawed by him. I had no idea how he would react to my plans. In fact, he was overwhelmingly supportive and wrote the following letter of commendation to Bishop Spong:

My dear Bishop,

Miss E. J. Canham

Miss Canham has asked me to commend her to you. This I gladly do. I ordained her to the diaconate on 1 October, 1978. She was ordained in Southwark Cathedral alongside the men. I make no distinction in the Ordination Service between man and women. I call the women deacons and not deaconesses and they are entitled to wear stoles. She is therefore a properly ordained deacon of the Anglican church. I wish it were possible for me to ordain her to the priesthood but as you know it is forbidden for the time being. I deplore the attitude of the Church of England but at least I am thankful that my successor, Ronald Bowlby, now Bishop of Newcastle, is the Chairman of the Council of the Ordination of Women.

Miss Canham has done good work on the teaching staff of the Church Army. She has been a lecturer in New Testament Studies on the Southwark Readers Course. She is also a non-stipendiary deacon on the staff of St Luke with Holy Trinity, Charlton.

I hope you will receive her into your diocese and in due course ordain her to the priesthood.

I resign my bishopric on 1 November and I suggest that if you want further information you write to me before that date.

 Kind regards,
  Yours very sincerely,

   (signed) MERVYN STOCKWOOD

From my conversations with some of the first American women priests, I had become aware of the need for support in the step I was taking since it would inevitably result in opposition from certain quarters. I therefore invited fourteen clergy and lay people, friends with whom I had worked and who I could trust, to meet together as a support group. We gathered in September and as I shared with them my hopes and fears we committed ourselves to work together towards my priesting. Some were members of the

Movement for the Ordination of Women, others had not previously been involved in the issue of women priests, but wanted to affirm me in my vocation.

The formation of the group marked a very important step for me. It not only provided a much needed sense of solidarity, but represented a personal recognition of my own value. Women have been slow to make claims for themselves and have often been plagued by a sense of guilt when they have done so. This is especially true in the church where the highest female virtue is most often represented as meekness and fulfilment through a supporting role to the clergy.

After the American House of Bishops' meeting, Bishop Spong wrote inviting me to return to Newark to test my vocation and suggested I send other letters of recommendation from people in England. At this point Katrina Swanson, whose vestry had invited me to be an assistant at St John's at an annual salary of $1, generously offered a place to stay and minister. The Church Army granted me two month's sabbatical leave and on Thanksgiving Day (27 November), I was back in the United States.

Before I left England I met with the Bishop of Southwark designate, Ronald Bowlby, (Bishop Mervyn retired on 31 October) since John Spong wanted to know whether he would endorse his predecessor's commendation. We met at St Edward's House, the London home of SSJE (Cowley Fathers) during General Synod week, since we both knew the house well. I knew Bishop Bowlby had been a supporter of women priests and was glad to find him a sympathetic listener and wise counsellor. He also wrote to Newark in support of my vocation to priesthood.

During December and January I served as a deacon in the diocese of Newark, primarily at St John's, Union City, under licence of Bishop Spong, and met with the Commission on Ministry and Standing Committee who approved my ordination to the priesthood subject to the completion of Canon 13 (on overseas clergy). This included examination in American Church History, Polity and Canon Law, as well as medical and psychiatric screening. I found the latter of great value and am convinced that the Church of England would have far fewer casualties if it required a similar examination of ordinands. The process lasted two full days and included psychiatric and psychological testing, career evaluation, and interviews.

On 28 January during the mid-week Eucharist in All Saints Chapel at Cathedral House, I was formally received as a deacon of the Episcopal Church in the USA. This was not an ordination to the diaconate, for Bishop Spong fully accepted Bishop Stockwood's declared intention in ordaining me deacon in 1978. I was presented to the Bishop for reception by the Revd Katrina Swanson and two members of the St John's Vestry, Pauline Luton and Mary Buess, and by the Revd Sanford and Mrs Dorothy Cutler, (Sandy had tutored me in American Church History and he and Dorothy provided generous hospitality while I was working on the examination). After the Bishop had established by question and answer that my Presenters were satisfied that all the canonical requirements had been met and that they believed my 'manner of life to be suitable to the continued exercise of this ministry', I made the declaration of assent. Bishop Spong then received me with the following words:

> Elizabeth, we recognize you as a deacon of the Anglican Communion, and we receive you into the fellowship of this Church. God the Father, God the Son, and God the Holy Spirit bless, preserve and keep you. Amen.

The Eucharist then proceeded as usual with intercession in litanic form including prayers for the Archbishop of Canterbury, the Bishop of Southwark, and my own ministry. Bishop Spong had already written to the Archbishop of Canterbury to ensure that he was fully informed of my transfer.

I was able to remain in America just long enough to attend the Annual Diocesan Convention from 30-1 January, and took a flight back to London that evening (though British fog kept us grounded at JFK airport for three hours!). I had no idea how I would be received on my return to England, officially as the Revd

Elizabeth Canham, though I suspected there would be some opposition. At this time I especially valued the Support Group and looked forward to sharing with them the experiences of those two months. At my request the Principal of the College had informed students of what had transpired during my Sabbatical but how they would react was unknown. The Church Army is not known as a radical institution — at least in its present form — and many of the students were theologically conservative, some vehemently opposed to women priests. I was to continue teaching that academic year and then return to America, where I was now 'canonically resident' in the diocese of Newark.

On the way in to my flat I met a member of staff who was opposed to the priesting of women. I was wearing a clerical collar and was surprised and encouraged by her hug and welcome. Her warmth and acceptance continued over several days and meant a great deal to me. Eventually I thanked her for her understanding and she said, 'I don't understand what's happening to me but as soon as I saw you I knew it was all right'. Over the next few months I was to experience, again and again, a similar reaction; people who had earlier been opposed to the ordination of women changing their position or at least rethinking because they encountered a person, not an argument.

On my desk in college was a hand made card illustrating contemporary America and pilgrims aboard the Mayflower. Inside it read, 'Like the Pilgrim Fathers you have stepped out in the courage of your convictions, for this we admire and respect you. You have our prayer support. God Speed'. It was sent by a student, who has declared she will leave the Church of England when women are priested in it! Amongst the student body I received acceptance and understanding even from those who could not share my views and who felt uncomfortable that I was already on the way to priesthood.

One colleague, a young Anglo-Catholic priest, did indicate his disapproval by avoiding me for the first few days. On the Monday following my return I was due to preach at college choral evensong and decided to give some background to the events leading to my reception as a deacon in America. I called the sermon, 'Mosaic' and the following is an excerpt from it:

'Lord, thou hast been our dwelling place in all generations' (Ps. 90.1). God is the home of his people. Sometimes it has been very difficult for them to hold on to that belief, especially when, through oppression or disaster, the structures which make for stability in life are torn away. Structures are important. The temple was important but in the course of time the structure became identified with God himself, and with the destruction of the temple came despair and hopelessness. God no longer had a 'home', and it took the insight and courage of men like Jeremiah and Ezekiel to convince the exiles that God had not abandoned his People. He was there with them in the far country, still their home, still leading them to new perceptions of his reality. Like Jacob centuries earlier running away from the chaotic mess his deceptions had created, they came to understand, 'Surely the Lord is in this place; and I did not know it' (Gen. 28.16).

We all unconsciously create for ourselves structures in which we feel comfortable and where God seems most accessible to us. Sometimes those structures become idols which we guard jealously, fearful lest someone come along and snatch away our source of security. And God becomes so closely identified with the structure that when it *is* removed we experience a sense of bereavement, loss and despair. Yet it may be that very loss which teaches us again that our only absolute security lies in God, not in particular forms of worship, places of prayer or among congenial people who believe as we do.

On the last occasion when I preached in college chapel, I talked about kaleidoscopes, and tried to say something about how all the fragments that make up our total experience, sometimes 'come together' in a remarkable way so that we see a pattern and symmetry in our lives. Tonight I would like to speak of 'Mosaics'. There is a certain randomness about how and when the shapes come together in a kaleidoscope. But if you are going to make a mosaic you have to be selective, to make decisions about which pieces you will place in the picture and where you will put them. You have to take some risks, to try out some bits which turn out to look wrong afterwards. Then it's an effort to chip away the cement, remove the piece and start again.

I believe we have some responsibility for designing the mosaic of our lives. Using our God-given powers of reason, seeking to be sensitive to the leading of the Spirit, and sometimes stepping out in faith when we are not sure, the picture is created. We have some risking to do as Christians, we are people called to live dangerously and when we make mistakes to deal with them and prayerfully move on.

This kind of risky living will involve us in some dark, painful moments, and it is important to pick up those pieces and see whether they contribute to the whole. Remember, the mosaic of Easter includes pieces taken from Gethsemane and Calvary. Christ took a huge risk which, for him, at the end seemed like failure, though we who live in the post-resurrection era see it as the definitive and central point in salvation history. In this risk taking, as we see ourselves bearing some responsibility for the shape of our lives, we discover God as our dwelling-place, our house of unshockable security.

I went on to relate the events which had led to my vocation being tested in America, my sadness at the prospect of leaving the college and England, and my hopes for the future.

The following Wednesday I was leading the Ministry of the Word at the midweek Eucharist, and my Anglo-Catholic colleague was celebrant. When it came to the administration he handed me the paten instead of the chalice and said, 'A gesture, Liz'. There was an audible gasp from some of the congregation — he had previously said no one but the celebrant would administer the host if he was presiding — and I found myself offering the Body of Christ to communicants through a mist of tears. It was not unusual for me to be administering the Host; I did it regularly in my parish where we used two altars for the main Sunday Mass, but in this context it represented a huge concession. I believe he was not only saying that he was prepared to acknowledge my vocation even if he still could not approve of women priests, but was also giving to me what was of highest value to him.

One of the first public events I attended after returning to England was the enthronement of the new bishop of Southwark. Originally I had been very uncomfortable about women wearing clerical collars, since some of those I saw initially accompanied them with very masculine attire. I have long been convinced that it will be a disaster if women who are priests simply move into the male hierarchical structures and models of priesthood. We have a joyful opportunity to discover new dimensions of a whole priesthood. The dog-collar seemed too masculine. However, as I looked for some other visible, easily identifiable sign, and as I saw young, attractive women tastefully combining a version of the clerical collar with feminine garments, I changed my view. Hence I attended the enthronement wearing my collar and received looks of incredulity, hostility, and delight. As I left the Cathedral I was embraced by the suffragan bishop of Kingston, who expressed his congratulations and delight.

Later I was to learn that one of the canons, a priest whom I knew well and with whom I had worked closely, had told friends that he disapproved of my coming to the cathedral deliberately to attract comment, and said I had chosen a prominent position to stand afterwards in order to create discomfort! I felt sad, not only because he had misinterpreted my action, but because he felt unable to express any of his disapproval to me personally. He was one of the signatories of the letters to Bishop Spong asking him to ordain me! I encountered a similar silence from a number of other clerics in the Diocese. They told friends that they were 'for' the ordination of women but 'against my way of going about it'.

So I began to find that some who felt the pressure of unresolved tensions within, chose to unload discomfort on me rather than deal with the problem. I have already indicated that some of the greatest understanding came from opponents of women priests, not from those who I thought were friends. This was especially true in relation to our other suffragan bishop, the Rt Revd Michael Marshall, known widely as a leading and vocal opponent of the priesting of women. He wrote warmly after I got back to England. Unfortunately, at this point the Press began to report what I was doing. Such headlines as, 'Battling deaconess to be ordained' and 'Holy Liz fights the good fight' appeared in the more sensational papers.

In March I went to Lambeth Palace to meet the Archbishop of Canterbury. He had already given permission for me to officiate as a deacon of the American Episcopal Church during the months before my return to America. Once admitted to the gatehouse and my credentials checked, I took the long walk across a courtyard and through the huge double doors, where I was met by the Archbishop's secretary. She warned me that TV cameras were installed in the Palace because the BBC were filming a documentary called *Robert of Canterbury*. When Dr Runcie greeted me at the door of his study, he asked if I objected to our interview being filmed. I had come intending to talk very personally about my own sense of vocation to the priesthood and the pain felt by many women because of the refusal of the Church of England to act on its own convictions. It was an ordeal to anticipate going on public record for the things I might say, but I also felt it important that the position of women in the Church should be exposed to the media in this way, so I agreed.

Dr Runcie listened compassionately as I told him of how my sense of vocation had grown, of the frustration of not being able to respond to those who were asking me for a priestly ministry, and of the sense of pain at the rejection of women's gifts to the priesthood of the Church. I also made it plain that though I was going to America feeling very positive about the prospect of ministering there for a period, my roots were in England and there was a sense of exile involved. I spoke of my hope to return and, as a priest, to help in the difficult period of transition when the Church of England did reverse its current position. The American Episcopal Church had recently been asked to supply two women priests to Liberia, so that the church there could experience their priestly ministry for a year before it decided whether to ordain women. I felt that the Church of England's ban on women lawfully ordained overseas was not only an insult on the women, whose male colleagues were readily accepted in England, but resulted in an impoverishment. Here was an ideal opportunity for people to experience women's priestly ministry and to examine how far their 'theological objections' were based on prejudice before another vote was taken on the ordination of women here.

From the outset the Archbishop had restated his continuing opposition to women priests — on the grounds that such a move might damage ecumenical relations — but expressed himself willing to listen. He promised to go on 'agonizing' over the question, asked to be kept in touch with my movements, and assured me that there was no doubt in his mind that we would have women priests in the Church of England before long. He gave me his blessing and I rose to go, glad to be free of cameras, tape recorders and reporters.

An hour later I was in the London Hospital at the bedside of the Rt Revd Colin Winter, the exiled bishop of Namibia. We were due to have tea together at the Namibia International Peace Centre that afternoon but Colin had been readmitted to the hospital after a routine check-up following his third serious heart attack a few months earlier, and had left messages at the centre asking me to visit the hospital. In spite of his own pain, the frustration of being no longer active in the struggle for Namibian Independence, he was able to offer support and inspiration to others engaged in struggle. We talked together and as I was leaving he said, 'Liz, give me your blessing before you go'. I was stunned and discomforted — I had just been talking to the Primate of all England about my frustration at not being a priest, and now a Bishop was asking me to exercise that ministry for him! Colin went on to say, 'Look, you are a priest. Soon the Church is going to affirm your vocation and I'm just a worn out Bishop who needs your ministry now'.

A few days later he sent this poem which he had written for me:

THE COST OF DISCIPLESHIP

What you have received
is what He gave you
What you know
and feel is truth

He has inspired
that which compels you
now to leave
home and hearth and
loved ones
He has prepared for you
you: His strength
perfected in your weakness:
Your weakness perfect in his strength
as Deborah was
a prophetess in Israel
As Hannah sang out
her love song
with liberated heart
As Mary
stood immovable
with sword pierced heart
in pain wracked
vigil
so you must stand —
you can no other —
and roll away the stone
of man-made
guilt and fears. For
you are a priest
forever
let all acknowledge it
and recognize the flowering
of your womanhood
in each and every priestly deed.

'That which I received I also passed on to you . . .'

5 Ordination

The visibility of women in holy orders does more to dispel doubt and prejudice than volumes of rational argument. All of us fear change — unless we are the instigators of it — and the spectre of fear can terrify us into vehement opposition or frightened inertia. To some in Britain I was a sign of hope, to others the cause of acute embarrassment. Those who seemed most uncomfortable were people, mainly priests, who said they were in favour of the ordination of women. It became clear that their support was theoretical. A woman in holy orders raised their anxiety level to uncomfortable proportions. My appearance in England wearing a clerical collar was perceived as 'confrontational', and I was often greeted with an embarrassed silence.

Some women too found my action difficult. Those who had spent years striving for change through synodical government felt cautious about any event which might polarize opinion. I did not see our approaches to be necessarily in opposition; we need able politicians, but sometimes prophetic action is also called for. So often non-action in the Church has been justified on the grounds that conflict is to be avoided at all costs. We want change to take place slowly and with minimal disturbance, but history tells us this rarely happens. Each of us has a personal timetable, and the difficulty lies in perceiving the *kairos*[1] of God. For me the moment to act had arrived and though it carried with it a sense of going into 'exile', there was a liberating joy in knowing my vocation was to be fulfilled.

Early in May 1981 I was back in the USA for interviews at St David's Episcopal Church, Kinnelon, New Jersey. I was encouraged by the unanimous decision of the Vestry to offer me the appointment as Associate Rector since they had never had a woman on the staff and one vestry member did not support women priests. At that stage I was, of course, a deacon. I returned

44

to England with plans to move to Kinnelon when the college term ended in June but was kept waiting for a visa from October until late August. My year in South Africa proved to be the final problem, since extensive police checks were made on my 'records' there and this took three months.

Before my official 'Farewell' at St Luke's in Charlton, I spent time with each of the three bishops in Southwark, receiving understanding and support from them. This was the third occasion on which I had talked to the bishop of Woolwich about my vocation and the outcome of each of these meetings has been creative and positive for me. On this occasion we talked honestly together of our pain. I believe we listened to each other and affirmed the integrity from which we both held our convictions. We also discussed the things which unite us: a deep concern for a relevant spirituality; the importance of recovering a genuine Catholic theology in the Church; our longing to see an incarnational, resurrection faith made accessible to the unchurched masses in our day. He gave me his blessing and, shortly afterwards, wrote:

> Although I cannot share the conviction which leads you to go to America I want you to know very much that I share in the Spirit in which you are undertaking this decision and hope very much that our paths will cross for further dialogue about this whole matter on one side or other of the ocean.
>
> With all good wishes and every blessing,
>
> Yours ever,
>
> † MICHAEL WOOLWICH

At the end of the summer term, I left my post at the Church Army Training College. My last official function was to assist with the administration of Holy Communion in Southwark Cathedral at the Commissioning Service. The celebrant was the Archbishop of Canterbury. In spite of having his permission to function in England as a deacon, I received a message from the cathedral staff asking me to 'dress as a deaconess' for the occasion! This decision was conveyed to me through the Church Army

Officer responsible for arranging the service, who was acutely embarrassed by it. I replied that either I would appear vested appropriately as a deacon or someone else must take my place. Eventually the demand was rescinded.

On 27 June, 1981, the Farewell Eucharist was held. Tony Crowe, the rector, was celebrant at the High Mass, I was deacon, and another woman staff member, Dss Anne Hoad led the ministry of the word and acted as sub-deacon. The preacher was Fr Alan Cotgrove, prior of St. Edwards House in Westminster, who, as my spiritual director, had shared so much of my inner struggle to recognize and fulfil a vocation to the priesthood. He reminded us all that:

> Ordination does not confer instant perfection or ability. It teaches nothing of living, loving or the cost to be paid. It does not confer immunity to such things as stress, fear or the place and battle of faith and prayer in these settings.

He ended the address by saying:

> . . . this is what ordination is about: to be the helpless, the taught, the doubter, the payer of the cost of true prayer, to be the dying one in order to be able to live. You can be the martyr struggling to the altar each day, to the Confessional, to the Parish House, but if these things are missing I believe ordination is incomplete.
>
> I do not know what the theology of ordination will be. I only see that what is happening today to people like Liz, who, I know, understands a lot already of my words tonight, can be a real part of the truth of God's way. And when I see that, I have no option but to allow it, and see and follow how it is to grow.

Bishop Colin Winter, who was too ill at that time to be present, wrote a hymn as his offering for the occasion. It was sung joyfully to the tune of 'You'll Never Walk Alone':

> When the Spirit of God
> At Creation's birth
> Swept over the darkness of night,
> And at God's command

Ordination

A great dawn burst forth
As he thundered out, Let there be light!
This God who made heaven and earth with a plan
Said all he had made was good:
Affirmed
His design
At the apex of all
Both man and woman stood
Both man and woman stood.

As the prophets of old
Were inspired to proclaim
God's love for the weak and the poor
Men and women were filled
With the spirit of truth
In their struggle for justice to secure
A nation set free from oppressor's chains
Where rivers of righteousness pour;
Serve God,
Serve God,
As you stand by the weak
And you'll never stand alone,
You'll never stand alone.

When the Church of our God
Is renewed again
Through the strivings of women and men
And as each plays a part
And is free to express
What the Spirit is saying to them,
When the hungry are fed and the poor are led
To inherit the land of their birth,
Free us!
Free us!
From hatred and greed
Holy Spirit, set us free!
Holy Spirit set us free!

This same Spirit of God
Moves today as of old
Changing hearts as she makes all things new.

For she breathes her new life
In a world filled with strife,
As she calls every nation to renew
The earth with a vision of justice and peace,
Which Jesus proclaimed of old.
Let peace
Christ's peace
Inspire every heart
As we follow him alone
As we follow him alone.

Let peace
Christ's peace
Inspire every heart
As we follow . . . him alone,
As we follow . . . him alone.

That same hymn was sung for a second time at Colin's funeral service the following November.

After the Sermon, the congregation were addressed by the rector with these words, reminiscent of the ordination service:

CELEBRANT

Liz has been a deacon at St Luke's for nearly three years. Throughout this period she has been aware of her vocation to the priesthood, and this has been widely recognized by the Church.

Sadly, to be ordained a priest, she has to leave us and move to another branch of the Anglican Communion, since it is not yet possible for women to be priested in the Church of England. In taking this step, she has the full support of the previous and present bishops of Southwark.

Is it your will that she should be ordained to the priesthood?

PEOPLE

It is.

CELEBRANT

Will you uphold her in her ministry?

PEOPLE

  We will.

CELEBRANT

  Let us pray.

As we all knelt the *Veni Creator* was sung and after further intercession the Peace was exchanged.

At the end of the service we sang Fred Kahn's lovely hymn, 'Into the World', and as I followed the crucifer out alone, other women who felt a sense of vocation to the priesthood joined the procession, until nine of us gathered in the Churchyard to finish the hymn. The evening ended with a 'Pot Luck' supper at which the parish presented me with a chalice and paten.

After a long summer in England waiting to complete the formalities for my visa, I finally left Gatwick airport on 28 August. My welcome at St David's was warm and I preached in church for the first time on 6 September. The complementariness of men and women working together in ministry became evident during my time at St David's. The rector and I brought very different skills to the church. He was 'called' by the congregation for his gifts in working with young people, and his enthusiasm and spontaneity make for a lively ministry. My own training and experience lie much more in teaching, lay training and working with people in the development of prayer and spirituality. Although we shared the whole ministry of the parish, there was scope to pursue personal interests. On the first occasion we shared together in conducting a wedding service, we became aware of the powerful symbolism of a male and female priest solemnizing a marriage.

For four and a half days each week I worked in the parish (my appointment was part-time). Two days were spent in New York at the General Theological Seminary, where I began work on a Master of Sacred Theology degree in Spiritual Direction. For some years in England I had been acting as director to several lay people and clergy but without any formal training. Obviously counselling training was a help, and I had been receiving spiritual direction for six years, but I knew of nowhere in the UK, which offered supervision and training in the skills required. My new group of 'directees' comprised members of the parish and seminarians from New York.

My ordination to the priesthood was set for 5 December, 1981, a year after I had come to the USA (as required by the Canons). The Press had begun to show some interest in the event and a TV company from England planned to be present as well as many visitors from the USA and Britain. The bishop suggested that the cathedral in Newark (twenty-five miles away) would be a more suitable venue than St David's, because it is far more spacious and accessible. Obviously the people at St David's were disappointed that I was not to be ordained among them in Kinnelon, but they accepted the decision and were thoroughly supportive. Three receptions were planned; one at Cathedral House immediately after the ordination, another a dinner that evening for members of the vestry, their spouses, visitors from England, and close friends, and a third for the St David's congregation, following my first celebration of the Eucharist next day. Two buses were chartered to take all those who did not want to drive to Newark, and several families opened their homes to my friends who were flying from England for the ordination.

The December issue of *The Voice* (the Newark diocesan paper) carried the headlines, 'Elizabeth Canham: First Englishwoman Priest. Newark shows Canterbury the Way!' Other local papers took up the story, and the religious affairs correspondent for the *New York Times* came to interview me. I did some preliminary interviews with the Independent Television 'Credo' team, who were in New York to film the ordination for a series they were preparing on women in society and in the Church. A press conference was set up at Cathedral House to take place the day before the ordination, so that I could be free to be with visitors after the service itself. I had invited Bishop Mervyn Stockwood to preach at my ordination, so with Bishop Spong and myself he faced the onslaught of questions. I had taken several days of retreat at Holy Cross Monastery a week previously, knowing that the arrival of English visitors and all the media interest would make it impossible later. I had also spent an afternoon with Bishop Spong preparing for ordination, looking with him at the awesome step I was taking as we prayed and talked together.

Invitations to the service carried an illustration of Psalm 30.6 'Weeping may spend the night . . . but joy comes in the morning' (APB translations). It was originally designed by the Revd Elsa Wallberg, a priest in the diocese of Massachusetts, and showed several figures with raised arms and palm branches facing the sun. The central figure was wearing a chasuble. For me this represented a summary of the past years. There had been weeping and struggle; in England I had wrestled with ecclesiastical structures, clerical chauvinism, misunderstanding, rejection, and with my own inner yearnings and now, far from home yet among many of those who supported me in England, the morning of joy had arrived.

Cathedral House, from which the procession began, is situated three blocks away from the Cathedral and across a main road. (I have processed from there in the depths of winter with several inches of snow on the ground and more falling on our vestments!). The vestry members from St David's, my presenters, lesson readers and Oblationers, followed the first crucifer and acolytes, and then came about fifty clergy from the diocese. I immediately preceded the second crucifer and the two bishops with their chaplains. As we walked, we were besieged by TV cameramen. We entered the Cathedral to strains of 'Hail thee, festival day', the singing being led by the choir of St David's.

Bishop Spong rose to make the following statement when the hymn ended:

> We welcome you to this historic moment in the life of the Diocese of Newark and of the entire Anglican Communion. We are pleased that each one of you could come to this State for this solemn and happy occasion. I specially welcome my brothers and sisters from the Church of England and from other traditions of Christ's one, holy, Catholic and apostolic church who are here to bear witness

to their convictions, and to stand in solidarity with women all over the world who endeavour to see the end of sexist discrimination in every branch of the Body of Christ.

To our pulpit, and to join me in the act of ordination, I welcome my esteemed colleague, the retired bishop of Southwark, the Rt Revd Mervyn Stockwood, who broke a barrier when he ordained Elizabeth Canham deacon in 1978 and who will become today the first Bishop of the Church of England to join in ordaining a woman priest.

The present Bishop of Southwark and my good friend, the Rt Revd Ronald Bowlby, was unable to be present but he has sent a statement which will be read on his behalf at the beginning of this service.

Bishop Bowlby's letter was then read by the Revd Tony Crowe:

Dear Elizabeth,

I have just realized that it was a year ago when we first met, and you told me of your belief that God was calling you to the ordained priesthood. Now all the processes of selection and final preparation are over, and you are approaching the day of ordination itself.

I want to say first what I would say to anyone about to be ordained, and that is to rejoice with you that you have been called and chosen to serve the church in this way. There was a time when people saw this as almost the only way in which someone could offer a full commitment to God. Now that is so no longer, happily. But it still remains a very particular and decisive step for you and for the church, one which I know you have not come to lightly or easily. You will need much grace, sensitivity and love in the years ahead, if you are to become the kind of priest that God can use for his purposes and the good of the whole Church. I want to assure you of my prayers and those of many in this Diocese as you go forward into this new ministry.

I want also to assure you of our support in the years ahead. You would have much preferred to be ordained to the priesthood in your own diocese and as a member of the Church of England. The decision to ask another part of the Anglican Communion to test your vocation and to give you employment has not been an easy one. Nor is it easy to be taking a step like this almost alone. For many women here who also long that the church will recognize that they have a true vocation, it is not even an option, as you well know. But I believe you made the right decision within your own circumstances, and that it will help more people in our own Church to recognize the personal reality that lies behind the Movement for the Ordination of Women. I hope it will not be long before you can be welcomed back to Southwark without restraint and conflict.

In one of your letters you write of 'incarnation' as the way forward for an acceptance of women priests, rather than abstract arguments. I am sure this is right, even though the discipline of clear argument is still needed as well. As we approach Christmas and the great festival of Our Lord's Incarnation, may your union with him be very close, and his priesthood and joy be yours in full measure.

Here are some words of St Augustine which have meant much to me over the years:

> Trust the past to the mercy of God;
> The present to his love;
> The future to his providence.

Have a happy and glorious ordination.

Yours in Christ,

RONALD

After the opening salutation and collect for purity, I stood before the Bishop with my Presenters. I had asked three clergy and three lay people from each of the two branches of the Anglican Communion, to which I had been affiliated, to present me for ordination. Two of the clergy from America were women; Suzanne Hiat and Alison Palmer, and the third was Sandy Cutler. Two of the lay presenters were St David's church wardens and the third was the vestry member, who was opposed to women priests when I arrived! I asked her because she had shown such warmth and support during my first months in the parish and I wanted to affirm that. However, the request came as a shock to her; she was still unable to accept the ordination of women, but said she loved and supported me so felt torn by my invitation. She thought and prayed about the decision for a week and then told me she was absolutely clear that she knew she had to say, 'Yes'.

Clergy presenters from the Church of England were my previous rector, Tony Crowe, Ian Ainsworth-Smith, the Chaplain of St George's Hospital, and David Gatliffe of St Paul's, Clapham, with whom I had taught on the Southwark Readers' Course. Three members of the support group, David Robson, Wendy Rhodes, and Frances Killick, were lay presenters, and the Revd Al Jousset completed the group. After I had been presented to the Bishop and made the Declaration of Assent, the congregation were invited to affirm their desire I be ordained priest and the litany for ordinations followed. The lesson readers also represented both Churches. Kath Burn, an Englishwoman training for the priesthood in New York, read the Old Testament lesson and was followed by two of the St David's lay readers leading the psalm and reading the epistle. Anne Hoad then read Colin Winter's poem (quoted on pages 42-3) and David Gatliffe was Gospeller.

Bishop Mervyn prefaced his address with a few carefully chosen words about the Church of England's statement that 'there are no theological objections to the ordination of women' and her slowness to act. He went on:

> Having ordained Elizabeth Canham to the diaconate for work in the diocese of Southwark, where, incidentally, in my time I have ordained nearly eight hundred priests, it had been my hope that she would have been among the eight hundred, but it was not to be.
>
> However, our sister church, the Episcopal Church of the United States, has provided her with the opportunity to be true to her vocation and I am deeply moved to think that my hands will provide the physical link between those two ordinations — hands which go out in love and fellowship to the Episcopal Church, to your bishop, and to you all.

The sermon was traditional, emphasizing the role of the priest as a herald, witness, envoy and teacher, and couched in heavily masculine language, which many of the women present found difficult to accept. It was a reminder to me of how much further the American Church has moved in using inclusive language, both in the liturgy and personal conversation.

Throughout the service I was surrounded by cameras and reporters, but at the moment of ordination their insensitivity to the occasion was most evident. One even climbed over the communion rail to get a picture. Fortunately, I was oblivious to much of it for I had determined to hold on to the solemnity of the occasion, the reality of God, and my vocation being affirmed by the Church. Just before the laying-on-of-hands, Bishop Spong reached down and took my hand and our eyes met during the time of silent prayers for which he had appealed. Those were profound, lasting moments for me before the clergy came forward to join the two bishops in the imposition of hands.

> Father, through Jesus Christ your Son, give your Holy Spirit to Liz, fill her with grace and power, and make her a priest in your church.
>
> May she exalt you, O Lord, in the midst of your people; offer spiritual sacrifices acceptable to you; boldly proclaim the gospel of salvation; and rightly administer the sacraments of the New Covenant. Make her a faithful pastor, a patient teacher, and a wise counsellor. Grant that in all things she may serve without reproach so that your people may be strengthened and your name glorified in all the world. All this we ask through Jesus Christ our Lord, who with you and the Holy Spirit lives and reigns, one God, for ever and ever. Amen.

I had wanted to affirm lay ministry in some way at the service, and so asked two women lay readers, Wendy Rhodes from England and Joan Ludwig of St David's, to vest me in stole and chasuble. The Bishop handed me a Bible and invited me to give the Peace to the congregation. I concelebrated with the two bishops and at the end of the Service gave the blessing for the first time.

In spite of attempts to deal with the Press ahead of time, so that I could be free to talk to guests at the reception, I was met by a sea of cameras and requests for interviews as I came out of the cathedral. The BBC sent Martyn Bell from Washington with a film crew, so family and friends in England were able to see the ordination on TV news next day. The rest of the day passed like a dream: visitors, telegrams, receptions, telephone calls, messages, flowers. A Roman Catholic priest in Rome wrote to tell me he celebrated mass for me that day. Groups of sisters from Anglican and Roman Catholic orders were at the service and others sent letters of support. I began to hear that the Press all over the world had picked up the story and it was even reported in the *South China Morning Post*!

In England the occasion was marked by a service at St Michael and All Angels, Camberwell, coinciding with the ordination in Newark. Members of the Support Group joined the congregation — to whom I have preached several times — in a celebration which expressed their solidarity. The following day at St Luke's a service was held at the time I was celebrating my first mass at St David's. The English visitors were present in Kinnelon, Ian Ainsworth-Smith preached and Tony Crowe brought greetings from England. He reminded us that by Greenwich Mean Time (*chronos*) London is five hours ahead of New Jersey, but in terms of *kairos,* the right moment to act, in ordaining women Britain was sadly far behind!

6 *Walls of Jericho*

In the final months before I left England, BBC Television screened a drama series entitled *The Walls of Jericho*. It told the story of Sophia Jex-Blake, and the struggle of women to train and practise as doctors at a time when suffrage and equal educational opportunities were denied them. British medical schools and universities were closed to women but when her friend, Elizabeth Garrett-Anderson, was ready to give up attempts to train in Edinburgh, Sophia began campaigning on her behalf. Eventually her frustration with the intransigence of those holding power in academic circles in Britain led Sophia to cross the Atlantic to make a tour of educational establishments in America. She had heard that women were accorded a much higher status in that country and soon she found this to be true. For a period of time she worked in Lucy Sewall's hospital in Boston, and also met Dr Blackwell, one of America's pioneer women doctors. Both encouraged her to remain in the country and train and Sophia became convinced that she too had a vocation to medicine. Her father's death resulted in Sophia's premature return to Britain, where she began to campaign with other highly qualified women for training and recognition. She encountered disappointment after disappointment but this did not curb her indomitable Victorian spirit, which refused to be satisfied with anything less than British women holding British medical degrees, practising medicine in their homeland.

I found many parallels with my own situation in the Jex-Blake story. The objections to women doctors, raised by males with a monopoly of the profession, were strangely reminiscent of General Synod! I too had made a transatlantic journey and found affirmation, but experienced a deep sense of exile. While her actions generated hope for some women, others were overcome by fear because she had dared to challenge the status quo by not accepting it without question. (Elizabeth Garrett-Anderson did not want to be a pioneer, was anxious to be regarded as 'feminine' and unaggressive, and was therefore unhappy with any 'crusade' for women doctors which might ruin her chances.) I too found that some women received new hope and energy when I returned to England for a brief visit, but others were afraid, and withdrew their support. I was also aware of the irony of another parallel; once again England was ruled by a woman (and now, in addition, had a woman Prime Minister), but women continued to be rejected as priests.

Even after women were admitted to Edinburgh University to study medicine, the battle was not over!

> It was as though all the reactionary, conservative forces which had seemed to treat the women's intrusion into the academic life a little indulgently as something which was only a passing whim, suddenly awoke to the fact that it was no whim but deadly earnest and that they were in grave danger.[1]

The women were subjected to verbal abuse, and, on their way to lectures, they were pelted with rotten eggs, disintegrating vegetable matter and horse dung. Having failed in their objective, the total exclusion of women from medicine, the opposition organized a powerful rearguard action.

By the time that I was ordained priest in America, there were women serving as priests in Hong Kong, Canada, and New Zealand as well as the United States. Australia had in principle voted in favour of the ordination of women, and two women priests were working in Liberia, so that the people of that country would have the opportunity to approve the priesting of women on the basis of their experience. From time to time women from these other Provinces of the Anglican Communion visited England, and frequently they celebrated House Eucharists, since the General Synod of 1979 rejected temporary legislation allowing legally ordained women priests to officiate even on a limited basis. Such services in private homes were a source of nurture and encouragement to those of us who felt impoverished by the Church's refusal to 'celebrate a whole priesthood'.

At the beginning of January 1982, I made a brief post-Christmas visit to family and friends in England, and agreed to celebrate the Eucharist in homes if I was invited to do so. One of the invitations I received came from the Dean of St Paul's Cathedral, the Very Revd Alan Webster, in whose home I had several times been present for an informal eucharistic celebration presided over by a woman priest. Alan's wife, Margaret, is the secretary of the Movement for the Ordination of Women, and they have both given warm support to those of us believed God was calling us to priesthood. Members of the Movement in the Metropolitan area were invited to be present for the celebration which was followed by a buffet supper. Some fifty or sixty people gathered — including a bishop and many priests — and it was for me a very moving experience to be celebrating in my own country for the first time, offering the Body and Blood of Christ to many who by their prayers and presence had supported my vocation. It was a moment tinged with sadness too, since several of those present came bearing the wounds of their own rejection, as they continued to ask the Church of England to test their vocations. I was little prepared for the intensity of the attack which followed later.

I was the celebrant at five such House Eucharists during this visit, one of them in the home of my previous rector at Charlton. On 3 January, I had preached in St Luke's and served as deacon at the Mass. Both Tony and the PCC had expressed regret that canon law prevented me from celebrating the sacrament in the church where so many had gathered to declare their support at my 'Farewell', and to express their desire that I be ordained to the priesthood. On the Feast of the Epiphany (6 January), a High Mass would normally have been celebrated in the church, but instead the congregation transferred the service to the Rectory and I was invited to preside. Surrounded by parishioners whom I had served — including some who initially were opposed to women priests — I rejoiced to share Eucharist, to see Christ's 'Epiphany' in our midst.

No doubt the fact that I was the first Englishwoman to transfer as a deacon to another branch of the Anglican Communion for ordination to the priesthood explains some of the intense media interest I attracted. (I am *not* the first British woman to become a priest, nor the only one to seek holy orders elsewhere, as some erroneously reported.) No doubt also the presence of so many British clergy and laity at the ordination and, in particular, the presence of my previous diocesan bishop who shared in the laying-on-of-hands, made it even more noteworthy. During the two weeks in England I was besieged with requests for TV and radio interviews, and also by the Press. It was exhausting, but I was glad that so many people were made aware of the Church's 'apartheid' policy at this time.

As soon as I arrived back in the USA the 'reactionary, conservative forces' began to operate. Letters, telephone calls, statements poured in to the Diocesan Office, to my apartment, and to St David's. The following letter, presumably from a priest since it came from a vicarage, is one example:

Dear Madam,

The essence of Christianity is obedience emanating from love of the Father (St Luke 22.42). Discipleship implies discipline. Your parading around London brandishing the Blessed Sacrament as a ? of defiance exhibits none of the traits. Activity of this type stems from pride. Such activities offend the susceptibilities of other people, which is an offence against Agape — not the superficial 'mush' exhibited in so many ecclesiastical circles today alongside a superficial theology.

The 'serpent' remains . . . more subtle than any beast of the field . . . and knows how best to thwart God's plans, and is having a great deal of success in these days.

In a 'Church Times' article by Douglas Brown, 29 January 1982, an otherwise positive statement entitled, 'Challenges on our attitudes to Women' contained this sentence:

It is, of course, offensive to many to use the Eucharist, as Miss Canham has done, as part of the razzmatazz of protest and persuasion.

How a quiet celebration of the Eucharist in a private home for those who were already persuaded that women may be priests could be described as 'brandishing the Blessed Sacrament' or 'part of the razzmatazz of protest and persuasion' mystifies me. The offence must surely lie with those who perpetuate a discriminatory policy, which deprives many of a ministry for which they yearn.

On the day on which I arrived back in America, 12 January 1982, the Bishop of London issued a four-page statement to the London Area Bishop's Council. The statement was embargoed until 5.00 p.m. on that day. I first knew of it through a British journalist who called me long-distance to ask for my reactions to Dr Leonard's 'condemnation of the Eucharist celebrated in St Paul's Deanery'. Obviously I could offer no comment since I had not received the statement and knew nothing of its specific contents. I had been in London for an entire week after the Eucharist, and no objections had been expressed to me or to the Dean during that time. Now, when I was four thousand miles away, a statement was issued! Although sections of Bishop Leonard's document were quoted in the Church Times and other British newspapers, I did not receive a copy and did not see its contents until my bishop in the United States made it available to me. The statement focused on Canon Law and the interpretation of the Resolutions of the 1978 Lambeth Conference. The Bishop began by stating that:

> . . . the law both of the Church and of the land leaves us in no doubt that anyone who has been legally ordained abroad is not allowed to perform any ecclesiastical function in the Church of England, whether privately or publicly, without, first, the authorization of the Archbishop of Canterbury under the Overseas Clergy Measure and, secondly, the authorization of the bishop of the diocese.

This law, often referred to as the Colonial Clergy Act (which gives an indication of its date and purpose), is interpreted very loosely when male priests visit England. Many of my colleagues in America assure me they were not even aware of it, and even those who have spent a considerable amount of time in England on clergy exchanges, have found that their transfer to an English diocese took place with minimal formality. Another issue raised by the Bishop's opening statement is whether a House Communion among friends can be called 'an ecclesiastical function in the Church of England.'

The Resolutions of the Lambeth Conference were intended to enable those provinces of the English Communion, which do ordain women priests and those who do not, to co-exist in mutual respect and charity. The Bishop of London claimed that a non-proselytizing service in a private home violated those Resolutions. He went on to record that the Anglican Consultative Council was requested:

> . . . to use its good offices to promote dialogue between those member Churches which ordain women and those which do not, with a view to exploring ways in which the fullest use can be made of women's gifts within the total ministry of the Church in our Communion.

I find very little evidence to suggest that this request has been taken at all seriously. At least the issue was raised following this celebration, though sadly many voices were strident. Some debate has taken place since. My own bishop's response, which I record later, and his appeal for dialogue, represents an attempt to begin talks. Archbishop Ted Scott of Canada also appealed in writing, and later in person at General Synod, for some movement in the Church of England. Much as I regretted being the centre of controversy, I was glad that the issue had again been raised and was being discussed. The statement by Bishop Leonard ended by saying:

> Elizabeth Canham is canonically resident in the diocese of Newark, USA and is responsible to the bishop of that diocese as her ecclesiastical authority. I propose sending him a copy of this statement and referring the matter to him. I am also sending a copy to Lambeth to await the Archbishop of Canterbury on his return from the Far East asking that he will seek to dissuade others from acting in a way which is not in accordance with the Lambeth

Resolutions and which thereby causes distress and dissension within the Anglican Communion.

Once again, media interest was intense and editorials, articles, and letters began appearing in the religious and secular press. Since I was not in England, and saw none of these until some time after publication, I did not respond personally to any of them. However, when *The Living Church,* the major weekly publication of the Episcopal Church in America, published an article accusing me of celebrating a schismatic rite, '. . . in defiance of the Bishop (of London) and in defiance of the canons of the Church of England (14 February)', I wrote to the editor. He had also claimed that my ministrations in England were unnecessary, since the nation was filled with half-empty churches. My reply was published on 21 March and I quote it in full since it addresses some of the issues raised by Bishop Leonard's statement:

Dear Sir,

I write with reference to your editorial "Schismatic Rite in London" (*TLC* 14 Feb.). Your comments contained a number of inaccuracies which I would like to bring to the attention of your readers.

I did not celebrate in London 'in defiance of the bishop of that city' and in no way anticipated that a House Eucharist would be subject to episcopal ecclesiastical discipline. The *Church Times* carried a report that the celebration at St Paul's Deanery was one of several such services which I had been asked to conduct during my visit. This statement appeared several days before the celebration, and I was in London for a week after it had taken place.

At no point during that time were any objections raised by the bishop of London, either to me personally or to his dean who issued the invitation. Only on the day I arrived back in the USA, was any displeasure publicly expressed in London. On a number of occasions I have been present at similar services conducted by women priests from New Zealand and America for those of us who felt deprived of the sacramental ministry of women. These were not subject to episcopal discipline.

On a regular basis in the London diocese and elsewhere such 'uncanonical' services as Benediction take place and are publicly advertised. I do not have problems with this or with the precedents set by the Oxford Movement at a time when the Church of England forbade a full expression of the Catholic faith. On frequent occasions, I have attended Solemn Evensong and Benediction at All Saints, Margaret Street, London. However, I do question the bishop's selective use of the 'law' to oppose what he does not like.

You also suggest that, since the nation is filled with half-empty churches, my ministrations were not necessary. Those who came to the five House Eucharists at which I was celebrant (about 150 people in all) were present because, for them, a priesthood which is all-male is incomplete. They chose to avail themselves, in people's homes, of an opportunity denied them in the churches.

One of the reasons for our half-empty churches is that, for many people, the Church of England has lost credibility. The decision not to ordain women priests in spite of the General Synod statement in 1975 that '. . . there are no fundamental objections to the ordination of women' contributed to this sense of disillusionment.

One woman received communion for the first time in many years at the celebration in the Deanery, and there are many men and women whose integrity has compelled them to withdraw from the institutional Church.

The present attitude of the Church of England towards women priests ordained elsewhere in the Episcopal Church raises the question of the reality of the 'Anglican Communion'. Naturally, I feel devalued by the non-acceptance of my priestly ministry in England, but I am also embarrassed by the question mark this places against my bishop since it appears also to call into question his episcopacy.

After he had had time to read and digest the Bishop of London's statement and request that he take action as my 'ecclesiastical authority', Bishop Spong issued a response. This was first mailed to the Archbishop of Canterbury and the Bishop of London so that they would have copies before it was made available to the Press. Bishop Spong then read his statement in Trinity Cathedral, Newark, where a few months earlier he had ordained me to the priesthood.

'I am in receipt of the statement of 12 January issued by the

Bishop of London, the Rt Revd Graham Leonard, protesting the celebration of a house Eucharist by the Revd Elizabeth Canham, priest of the diocese of Newark. I have also read in the *Church Times* the reaction of the Archbishop of Canterbury, the Most Revd and Rt. Hon. Robert K. Runcie, to the same event. In this statement I would like to respond to each.

The Bishop of London cites "the law of the land and the law of the Church" that make it illegal for anyone ordained abroad to perform any ecclesiastical function "in the Church of England" without the authorization of the archbishop of Canterbury and the bishop of the diocese. This is a legalism that results from being the established Church, which in a pluralistic society appears increasingly anachronistic.

The assumption the Bishop of London is making here is that every service performed within the geographical boundaries of his diocese is a service performed 'in the Church of England'. This assumption is not made in all quarters of the Church of England and has been publicly disputed by the Bishop of Birmingham. Strictly observed in its most literal interpretation, Roman Catholic priests or Scottish Presbyterian pastors would then have to have the consent of the Anglican bishop of London to have a home communion service within his cure. To suggest that the Revd Elizabeth Canham performed an ecclesiastical function "in the Church of England" by conducting a house Eucharist stretches the concept of the established Church to a breaking point.

It should be stated clearly that Miss Canham was the guest of the Very Revd Alan Webster, dean of St Paul's Cathedral, who invited her to celebrate the Eucharist in his home. If ecclesiastical consent was necessary, surely it was the responsibility of the host, not the guest, to see that all was in order. Clearly Dean Webster did not feel that he was acting inappropriately, or else he felt that the issue was of such import that bending the requirements was justified.

There are, however, deeper issues here that need to be faced. Let us assume for a moment that the most rigid legalistic interpretation is made of what Bishop Leonard calls "the law of the Church and the law of the land." The fact would still remain that this law has always been most generously interpreted by officials in the Church of England. Mutual recognition of the ministry of each branch of this communion has bound us together. At this moment a priest from our diocese of Newark works on the staff of the bishop of Chelmsford. Clergy exchanges have occurred numerous times between our Episcopal clergy in Newark and England's clergy. The Bishop of Liverpool and the Bishop Retired of Southwark have very recently been the honoured guests of our diocese.

These exchanges have always been accomplished in a most routine and gracious way. I certify to the English bishop or he certifies to me that the priest is in good standing. Nothing more is required. Now suddenly the presence of a priest from Newark who has deep English roots is the cause of alarm and the great outpouring of energy. Surely it is obvious that there is only one reason for this, and it is not the issue of a house communion service. It resides solely in the fact that the Revd Elizabeth Canham is a woman. Because she is a woman, the letter of the law is applied, legalistic arguments are used, and what would once have been so minor an event as not to be noticed is the occasion of a four-page statement by the Bishop of London and a press release from the Archbishop of Canterbury.

I respect the decision-making process of the Church of England even though I disagree with the result of that process on this issue at this moment. The Church of England must also respect the decision-making process of the Episcopal Church. Though many see Elizabeth Canham's ordination as a prophetic sign aimed at England, her ordination did not occur for that reason. She was ordained rather because after a vigorous screening and testing process we affirmed her vocation as one whom God has called and endowed for the priestly office. All I ask is that the Church of England accord to her the same courtesy, the same acceptance, they would accord any other Episcopal priest when she is a guest in England.

Miss Canham is fully employed as a curate at St David's Church in Kinnelon, New Jersey. She will be in England only for short visits to see her family. She is not planning at this time to move to England to start a crusade. She does not desire to violate church law or take over church altars. She has never functioned as a priest in a place to which she was not invited. Hers is not a militant, controversial nature. She is an Englishwoman who loves her native land and her Mother Church. She would welcome the day when she could once again be a part of both.

Large numbers of clergy and communicants of the Church of England stand ready to invite her into their worship. The leadership of the Church of England is aware of these supportive people. They will not be silent, and they will not go away. The future belongs to them. In a country where Elizabeth II is Queen and Margaret Thatcher is Prime Minister, it is particularly evident that women are taking their full and rightful role in every aspect of the life of the world. The Church will be no exception to this mighty tide of change.

The leadership of the Church of England must know that they cannot recognize some Episcopal clergy and not all Episcopal clergy. If the Church of England is not willing for our women priests to function sacerdotally in England on any occasion, they must not allow our male priests to do so either. Should that tragic day come to pass, then the American Episcopal Church would, it seems to me, have to take a similar position. Reciprocity and mutual recognition of the ministry of each autonomous national branch of the Anglican Communion is an essential ingredient in our corporate life, and without it the very matrix of the Anglican Communion is broken.

I hope the Bishop of London, who is well known for his opposition to the ordination of women, will weigh well the full dimensions of the attitude his statement expresses. Beneath the concern for the technical details of 'the law of the Church and the law of the land' lies, I submit, the very life and future of the Anglican Communion.

I was further saddened and a bit surprised at the statement on this event made by the Archbishop of Canterbury and published in the *Church Times.* Dr Runcie is a gracious man whose friendship I treasure and whose honest candour I have welcomed in our correspondence. I can only assume that he did not realize the manner in which his words would be heard in large segments of the Anglican Communion. Referring to his trip to the United States in 1981, he remarked that no one tried to 'embarrass' him by forcing him to function sacerdotally with women priests.

As the Archbishop of Canterbury, Dr Runcie is the spiritual head of the Anglican Communion. The Anglican Communion has women priests in the United States, in Canada, in New Zealand, in Hong Kong. If it is an embarrassment to function with a priest of the communion one heads, then the fiber of integrity that holds that communion together has been ripped asunder. That statement calls into question not just our women priests but the bishops who have ordained them and the General Convention of the Episcopal Church which authorized such ordinations. It is also deeply disturbing to all people who believe that establishment of sexual wholeness in the priesthood is imperative to correct the sexist distortions of history.

The Archbishop also expressed concern about ecumenical relations with Roman Catholics and Orthodox Christians. Ecumenical relations, however, cannot be improved at the price of the destruction of one's own communion. The Roman Catholic and Orthodox Churches will have to relate to the fact that the Anglican Communion has women priests if they want to relate to the Anglican Communion. Part of the vocation of the Anglican Communion is to witness against sexual oppression and sexual prejudice in all branches of Christianity. To court unity by preserving prejudice and oppression is an unworthy goal of any branch of this church of ours.

I do not relish a series of statements crossing the Atlantic with increasingly shrill tones. I would welcome rather an honest, searching, thoughtful public dialogue that could be carried in the church press for the edification of our entire communion. Should the Bishop of London or the Archbishop of Canterbury desire to create that kind of forum, I would be pleased to help facilitate it in any way possible. The issues of sexism and the integrity of our communion are extremely serious matters. They should be addressed in a sensitive, open, and caring manner.

JOHN S. SPONG

Bishop of Newark

Bishop Spong's statement was quickly picked up by the press internationally and even greater impetus was given to the issue of women priests being extended the same courtesy as male clergy, when Archbishop Ted Scott of Canada added his support. The front page of the *Canadian Churchman* (April 1982) carried the headline 'US Bishop condemns C. of E. policy' and went on to say that the Canadian Primate agreed with the points made by Bishop Spong who was 'pushing at the issue as a matter of conscience'. It further reported that the Canadian House of Bishops at its fall meeting would be asked to give full discussion of the situation of Canadian women priests visiting England. Archbishop Scott had, on previous occasions, claimed that the refusal of another Anglican Church to accept the ministry of women priests reflects on the ministry of those who have ordained them. He also believed that the bishop, as a symbol of unity, has responsibilities: 'In a pluralistic church he has to symbolize that community which is inclusive of all points of view.' He further agreed with Bishop Spong that open debate and discussion of these issues was called for. The front page article ended with these words:

> Should the Church of England take no action on overseas women priests this summer, Archbishop Scott forsees it emerging as a major issue between the Church of England and the overseas Churches with women priests.

The main Editorial dealt with the St Paul's celebration, setting it in its historical context and suggesting some hypocrisy in the disproportionate condemnation it evoked, while similar celebrations passed almost without notice. It also implied that the Canadian Church had waited for the 'dialogue' advocated by the Lambeth Conference in 1978, and been disappointed.

RIFT DEEPENS WITH C. OF E. OVER VISITING WOMEN PRIESTS

'Two years ago, at a public meeting in London, England, Archbishop Ted Scott criticized the stand taken by the Church of England and the Archbishop of Canterbury on visiting women priests.

He told his audience, members of the Movement for the Ordination of Women, that forbidding such women to exercise their ministry while in England was causing a rift in the Anglican Communion.

No one in authority within the Church of England made public response to the primate's remarks, and now, two years later, the rift is there to be seen.

In 1980 it was the New Zealand church which most resented the stand taken by the Church of England. Today that resentment is shared by the Episcopal Church and the Anglican Church of Canada, and has been clearly enunciated by Bishop John Spong of Newark.

As Archbishop Scott has pointed out, this is not just an issue affecting women. In denying women priests the privileges it offers their male counterparts, the Church of England is refusing to recognize the validity of female priesthood. This immediately raises questions about the ministry of the men who have ordained women priests (in the Canadian church, the majority of bishops), and about the authority of national church bodies which have legislated such ordinations.

For men like Bishop Spong and Archbishop Scott, it is becoming an issue of conscience.

If the Church of England were simply a national church, this might be no more than a local issue. But it is regarded (and regards itself) as the "Mother Church" of the Anglican Communion. As Roman Catholic priests want to visit Rome, so Anglican priests want to visit England, the birthplace of the denomination.

But rather than welcoming visiting women priests as part of the Church's diverse ministry, the Church of England acts as if it has to protect its people from heretical contamination. Yet in no known case so far has any woman wanted to celebrate communion in order to proselytize among the English. Rather, the women have sought to serve as priests among their own friends, family, and supporters of women's ordination.

The Church of England is at present upset — enough so that the Archbishop of Canterbury and Bishop of London issued lengthy statements — because of actions of a visiting woman priest, Rev. Elizabeth Canham, in London over New Year.

But the church's outrage is also somewhat hypocritical, for it is not the first time it has happened.

Three years ago Rev. Joyce Bennett, who was ordained in Hong Kong in 1972, acted as priest during a public ecumenical service in Oxford, England. She received front-page publicity for her actions which came only two weeks after the Church of England's

70

ban on overseas women. The Church of England made no official response.

Two years ago an American woman priest, living in London, admitted in the pages of this newspaper that she also celebrated communion in public places, with the foreknowledge and support of at least one English bishop. The Church of England chose to overlook what she was doing.

There doubtless have been several other instances.

It is time the Church of England regularized the status of overseas women priests. A Private Member's Bill, expected to come before the church's General Synod this summer, offers the opportunity. The women still will not have the same status as their male counterparts, according to the bill, and this is to be regretted. But at least they will be recognized as priests.

But if the Church of England does not respond the rift between it and some of the largest churches in the Anglican Communion will widen, and widen dramatically.

Bishop Spong says the English church cannot recognize some Episcopal clergy, but not all Episcopal clergy. If it forbids women to function as priests, then it must forbid men as well. And if that happens, the American church would have to take a similar position.

Archbishop Scott, who does not deliver ultimatums and who is known for virtually unlimited patience, now talks of this emerging as a major issue which must be dealt with. If the Church of England will not put this part of its house in order, the Canadian church will begin to exert pressure, and that pressure will come from a high level.

So far the Church of England has not responded to the overseas churches on this issue. Bishop Spong's stand is a matter of conscience for him, and he has presented his case logically and clearly. He has even offered to facilitate open debate on the issue.

Yet the only public response from the Archbishop of Canterbury and the Bishop of London has been "No comment."

The fact that the Church of England refuses to communicate with those who are most concerned about this issue, the fact that it apparently refuses to even acknowledge that the issue is increasingly one of conscience for many overseas bishops, gives little cause for optimism.'

The inhabitants of Jericho shut the gates firmly from within when the forces of Joshua surrounded the city. No doubt they were amused as well as frightened by the bizarre antics of the marchers. No doubt Joshua had difficulty persuading his people that it was worthwhile making fools of themselves in order to achieve final victory. But the walls *did* fall. Sophia Jex-Blake and her colleagues saw them fall in Edinburgh; that made the ridicule endured in the struggle worthwhile. The ecclesiastical walls of prejudice against women have begun to crumble. In some countries they have been breached, and those Provinces of the Anglican Communion which now have women in the priesthood, will continue to challenge the 'Mother Church' as long as her defences are shored up by intransigent oppression.

For many years I have had on my wall a poster depicting moonlight shining through almost leafless trees. The caption reads, 'Happy are those who dream dreams and are ready to pay the price to make them come true'. The words are taken from the reply given to a journalist by Léon Joseph, Cardinal Suenens, when he was asked why he was a man of hope. He answered that not natural optimism but a dynamic God who makes each day vibrate with new life, and who initiates the 'surprises of the Holy Spirit' was the ground of his hope. Impossible barriers are overcome, solid walls collapse, rigid tradition expands to embrace new insight and human self-understanding grows, as this God acts.

I know only too well the feeling of being shut out, of being the object of scorn and derision by those safely 'inside'. I know too, moments of elation, joy, and hope. I was shocked when some years ago a group of women sang, 'We shall overcome', following a Eucharist celebrated for the Christian Parity Group in England. It seemed altogether too militant and inappropriate in such a context. Now, knowing something of the struggle of black people in America, for whom that song became so important when they chose imprisonment and harassment rather than capitulation to unjust law, and having shared the struggles of women with a call to priesthood, I see that it precisely expresses the confidence I

72

feel. I do not want to minimize the pain, past and future, or suggest that there will not still be times of near despair when nothing seems to be happening. But I am certain that hope, not fear, must provide the energy to go on walking around the walls. For hope is one of the fundamental Christian virtues, and God goes on surprising us by the action of the Holy Spirit in our day.

7 *Not Me But Us . . .*

During July and August of 1982 I learned what it meant to be a 'recusant' priest. When Roman Catholicism was systematically suppressed in England in the sixteenth century, those who remained faithful to that communion, at least in private, received the sacraments from priests who went into hiding. In their homes Mass would be celebrated and confessions heard, and to this day there remain some 'priest's holes' constructed as hiding places. I spent two months ministering to groups of people in England that summer mostly in private homes, and responding to the sacramental and pastoral needs of those who invited me.

My feelings at this time were very mixed. First, it was affirming to know that my priestly ministry was much needed in England and that there were those who yearned to receive the sacraments from a woman. But I was also hurt because of the public rejection of that ministry by the Church which I loved, and I was torn by the invitation from one parish to celebrate at their main Sunday Mass; I longed to say 'Yes', since it was a church where I had had a growing pastoral relationship. When I declined, the PCC said that to ask me to do anything less than celebrate for them would make them feel they were devaluing my priesthood, and so I celebrated a House Eucharist in the rectory instead. On two occasions I did concelebrate at parishes where I was the preacher, and thankfully this was not the subject of press notice on this occasion.

While I was in London the General Synod met and two important debates were scheduled. The first concerned 'Covenanting for Unity' with the Methodist, United Reformed, and Moravian Churches. This had received the initial two-thirds majority in each of the Houses and had been referred to the Dioceses for discussion prior to the final vote. Now the lengthy process had ended and the Covenant, which would involve a mutual recognition of ministries and the acceptance of episcopacy by the other Churches, was to be accepted or rejected. I sat in the Visitors' Gallery listening to the debate and grew increasingly depressed as the day wore on. There was much talk of structures, hierarchies, models of ministry (much of it no doubt important), but little emphasis on mission, on sharing the Gospel with a world which cared little about denominational labels, or *being* Christ in the community.

When the vote was taken Bishops and Laity voted by a large majority to adopt the Covenant; the motion was lost in the House of Clergy.

The Covenant voting was as follows:

BISHOPS		CLERGY		LAITY	
Ayes	*Noes*	*Ayes*	*Noes*	*Ayes*	*Noes*
38	11	148	91	154	71
77.5% in favour		61.9% in favour		68.4% in favour	

N.B. The motion was lost in spite of a majority in each House.

It was a heavy blow, especially for those Churches who had experienced much internal conflict in the process of reaching agreement to accept the Anglican proposals. Sitting in the gallery with many clergy from these denominations I felt ashamed and embarrassed. My discomfort was even greater when, a few days later, I was recording two television interviews for Anglia TV, and discovered that the interviewer was the Area Moderator of the United Reformed Church. He was, of course, deeply disappointed, but very charitable in his attitude towards me and the Church of England.

If the Covenant proposals had been accepted this would have involved recognizing each other's ministers which, of course, include women in the 'free' churches. Undoubtably this was seen as a serious stumbling block by many and was one of the reasons for the negative vote. It would indeed have been unconscionable to accept the ministrations of women clergy from other churches, while continuing to reject the ordained women in our own communion. It would also have been a grave insult to the highly qualified deaconesses and other women in England who waited to have their vocations to the priesthood tested, though I believe many of them would have welcomed such a move.

I do believe that it is important to safeguard the priesthood and I also experienced some disquiet about certain aspects of the Covenant. In my final chapter I try to reflect on what the priesthood means to me after a year as a priest. There is such breadth of opinion about the nature of priesthood even within the Church of England, and each time the question of women priests is raised it is suggested that we need to define and clarify priesthood before acting. Somehow this priority quickly gets forgotten once the question has passed.

At noon the following day, Archbishop Ted Scott of Canada was invited to address the Synod. He did so with remarkable candour, inviting the Church of England to stop behaving like 'Aunty' to other branches of the Anglican Communion, and to recognize the insights and gifts which these Provinces have to offer. Among his appeals for changed attitudes he pleaded for a recognition and acceptance of women priests ordained in these churches. During the lunch recess the Open Synod Group arranged a meeting, inviting all Synod members to come and meet informally with the five women priests who were present. Caryl Marsh and I are both Englishwomen, and another American woman had received part of her training at Cuddesdon College, Oxford. To some we were curiosities, but many members were genuinely relieved to meet women priests, and to discover that we did not have horns and a tail!

Later that afternoon Deaconess Diana McClatchey presented a motion requesting Synod to instruct the Standing Committee to introduce legislation to enable women lawfully ordained to the priesthood in other Anglican Provinces to be given permission to exercise their ministry on particular occasions during temporary visits to the Provinces of Canterbury and York. She pointed out that, as predicted, the number of visits by women priests from overseas had increased, and this was why she was requesting further consideration of the issue. Her motion was less demanding than the one defeated in 1979, which would have resulted in a policy of extending to women priests the same courtesies as those offered to their male colleagues. Deaconess McClatchey was asking for a limited permission to be given to women to officiate on clearly defined occasions and felt the time for change had come. She said:

> Despite considerable pressure — and largely as a result of the firm line maintained by the Central Council of the Movement for the Ordination of Women — the law was not openly flouted. Communion Services were held in the open air, at ecumenical centres, in private houses as differing pastoral situations dictated. I took part in some myself. Blind eyes were turned: the occasions increased, tension grew, the media became interested, and *private* was suddenly glaringly *public.*
>
> The lawyers were again consulted: and as a laywoman I cannot argue with the rulings . . . But I can see, very clearly, the consequences. The Eucharist, the most solemn sacrament of our unity in Christ, became a source of argument and controversy, kicked about the market place by press and media like a cheap football, by individuals, who frequently did not even know the meaning of the word, and whose main concern seemed to be to stoke the flames of discord. And that *hurt* deeply: there is not an individual here I expect who did not find it equally distressing: equally distasteful. The irony is that no one — and most certainly not the celebrants — ever intended that a celebration of the Eucharist should become part of a political strategy, a demonstration, a propaganda pawn on the chessboard of ecclesiastical politics.

Deaconess McClatchey also confessed to her own conniving at a breach of the laws of the Church of England by attending Benediction when she lived in a North London parish, and reminded the Synod of disciplinary action taken against clergymen in the last decades of the nineteenth century, because they practised Anglo-Catholic rites. She then said:

> It is ironic that the spiritual descendants of the rebels against strict

interpretation of the law in the 1880s are today amongst those who insist that the letter of *this* law under question must *now* be observed. And even more deliciously ironic when we remember how overwhelmingly successful their own rebellion was.

I listened to the debate which followed and was glad that at least one opponent of women priests found the courage to say that the 'problem' would not go away. The Anglican Communion *has* women priests and it is important for the Church to find ways for them, and those who wanted their ministry, to co-exist with others, like himself, who utterly rejected it. When the vote was taken (by Houses at the request of an opponent) it was as follows:

BISHOPS		CLERGY		LAITY	
Ayes	*Noes*	*Ayes*	*Noes*	*Ayes*	*Noes*
24	4	106	68	103	60
85.7% in favour		61% in favour		63.1% in favour	

This reached the required simple majority but when the issue returns it will no doubt require a two-thirds majority in each House, and there is a likelihood of further delay if it is referred to the dioceses for discussion.

I left Synod knowing that, whenever I responded to pastoral needs while I was in England, I was technically breaking the law. Yet how could I refuse to exercise my priesthood when compassion and need demanded it? Was this not precisely the dilemma which Jesus faced when asked to heal on the Sabbath; when he defiled himself by eating with the rejected and 'unclean'; or when he pronounced healing and forgiveness?

The previous afternoon I had met a woman who asked me if I would agree to hear her confession and we made an appointment for later in the week. She had felt so deeply wounded by the Church and its rejection of women, that she no longer felt able to attend services or receive the sacraments from male priests. Although she felt excluded by the community into which she was baptized, she maintained a personal life of prayer but was acutely isolated and lonely. The Church was saying I might not give her absolution; my own inner conscience and vows as a priest made it impossible to refuse the request. Some time later I received a letter from her in which she told me that the Sacrament of Reconciliation had enabled her to be healed of her alienation from the Church. She wrote:

> The possibility of confession and absolution from a woman priest was critical. That possibility released me from excommunication — after an absolute shrinking, almost a sense of being terrorized in relation to the male priesthood. I made my communion . . . for the first time this year. I was querulous and uneasy in that event, but I was there. And it's been a hard won step back into some relationship with the rest of the Body.

Many of the groups who invited me to meet with them and to celebrate the Eucharist expressed deep gratitude for my ministry. A large proportion of those present were women, and I was often reminded of Sophia Jex-Blake's words to her students when they honoured her, 'Not me but us'. I felt a deep sense of solidarity with those whose vocations were unfulfilled, and all who supported and longed for women priests. They shared the struggle and for many who could not express a full priestly ministry in the Church of England, the pain was acute. I know that when I am present at a service where the celebrant is a woman, I somehow feel that my own priesthood and my personhood is being affirmed. I was glad that women in England could hear God saying 'Yes' to them through my priesthood.

For some, however, the experience of rejection as women with a vocation to priesthood, was made more acute by my presence. After all, I had 'achieved' what they longed for. I *was* a priest. Their feelings of frustration and envy were natural, and not all could handle the pain. I felt the deepest respect and sympathy for one deaconess who left a Eucharist at which Caryl Marsh was celebrant and I acted as assistant. She simply could not bring herself to receive communion from us, because of her unresolved resentment that we were priests. At another House Eucharist at which I was celebrant, a woman had said she did not think she could receive the sacrament from me because she was not sure whether I was American or English and so many English women were still unordained. She did not herself have a priestly vocation but was a strong supporter of other women who did.

There were inevitably some who considered that my 'style' of ministry was inappropriate. One woman priest who was also in England that summer later wrote to me saying:

> . . . keep fairly low key if you visit England in the near future. So many people with whom I had good conversations on the issue of women priests in the C. of E. had been put off by the challenges you were making.

Clearly she had 'heard' only what my critics said and had formed an opinion about me (we had never met), visualising me as strident, confrontational and 'unfeminine'. Since she had not lived in the country, or experienced the long history of rejection, she had not grasped the fact that simply by going overseas to be ordained I was perceived as confrontational. I did not 'make challenges' but as soon as I set foot in England, I represented a 'challenge' to the Church there. That kind of misunderstanding was more difficult to deal with than direct opposition.

I visited several religious communities that summer, celebrated Mass for one of them, and spent several days of Retreat at St Michael's Convent, Ham Common. It was very good to be back there again and to reflect on the previous nine months as a priest.

There were many memories of my first visit shortly after my ordination in Southwark Cathedral and the negative vote on women priests in 1978. While I was there this time, the Reverend Mother invited me to meet with the Sisters and tell them of my work in America, especially the studies in Spiritual Direction. Before I left, I was scheduled to lead a weekend Retreat there in 1983 and to offer a day workshop on Spiritual Direction for the Community. I was so appreciative of this invitation for it recognized that I was a priest with a particular ministry to offer and not just a spokesperson on the ordination of women. A few days before, I had led a Quiet Day organized by a group in the St Albans Diocese where I had grown up. That too had meant a great deal to me for the same reasons.

I returned to America with both regret and anticipation. On the one hand, though I had had a demanding itinerary in England, it was good to be 'home' and to be valued by friends and supporters. On the other, England had felt like a hostile place to be. Stony looks of hatred, which did not even acknowledge me as a sister in Christ, from several clergy-members in Synod, and the sense that many (including the media) were waiting for me to publicly break the law, made it a tense time. My return meant a move to New York City with all the noise and bustle that I had grown to love. It also meant a year of study, teaching and writing at the General Theological Seminary, while continuing my canonical residence in the diocese of Newark just across the Hudson River. (My temporary position as Associate Rector at St David's ended in June. Thus I was able to spend a substantial time in England before the Michaelmas Semester began.) And it meant risk and an uncertain future which filled me with excitement and panic. Nevertheless, when I finally arrived in the 'Big Apple' after a short holiday in Massachusetts, I knew this was where I should be.

8 *At the Edge*

As a child I was often told to come back from the edge. Standing on the platform as one of the old steam trains snorted its way into the station, or going as close as I dared to the swiftly flowing river near our home, I caused anxiety to those who were more cautious. In recent years I have learned to value people who have found the courage to live on the edge of Church and Society because that is where their convictions have led them. Through them I have been given a vision of what it means to live with integrity whatever the cost; to follow the radical Christ.

In his book, *America is hard to find,* Daniel Berrigan describes his experience as a resister following the burning of draft papers in protest against America's involvement in the Vietnam War. He went underground to avoid arrest and during that period, and subsequently from his prison cell, he wrote a collection of letters and reflections. He describes this experience as 'life at the edge', and finds history producing many examples of those who have lived there:

> Merton used to say that the monk is a man at the edge of both Church and society, barely tolerated by either; but being at the edge he has the inestimable advantage of being able to talk with those whose lives are a long pilgrimage at the edge, coming in, going out, pausing here, hoping there, despairing almost always. That edge where the future is both endangered and engendered. Bonhoeffer spoke of this too, his biographer said. Once he realized that he must live at the edge, he was a dead man in both Church and State, and knew it.[1]

I believe it was Käsemann who once wrote, '. . . grace means to have been a resister in a special situation.' Christians are called to be resisters of all that denies the gospel, to be signs of contradiction in a world which has got its values back to front. And that will drive them to the edge. It will also enable them to become God's free people, no longer bound by convention, fear or oppression.

The Revd Dr Martin Luther King Jr lived at the edge and died by an assassin's bullet. During Easter 1980 the film of his life was screened on British television and somehow spoke to me of resurrection far more powerfully than the complex liturgy we had just been celebrating. As I watched the film I jotted down some of the statements it made:

> There comes a time when people get tired of being trampled on by the iron feet of oppression . . . revolutions begin with hope not fear . . . privileged groups seldom give up their power voluntarily . . . we need a movement to reveal these people [whites] to themselves.

That was King; and from those who opposed change and a recognition of equality between black and white came the reply 'It isn't time to go ahead . . . You are going too fast . . . Congress isn't ready to act yet'. King insisted that there would be those for whom it was never the right time, and made it clear that the black people of America had waited long enough for their liberation and would not stop now. 'How long will prejudice blind the eyes of men? . . . truth will rise . . . I want to leave a committed life behind.' He was described by many as an 'impractical idealist' and a 'dangerous rebel' yet, through his breaking with neutrality, he made visible the gospel of freedom and hope. He stood at the edge with the man from Galilee, more free than his oppressors, more vitally alive than those 'wise' clergy and politicians, black and white, who urged caution and called for an end to the marches and boycott of the buses.

I think that I moved closer to the edge than ever before, when I finally left England and began my ministry in America. I had expected to be working in an urban, mission parish where problems of unemployment, poor housing and a high crime rate necessitated a practical outworking of the gospel. I found myself in a very beautiful rural area, surrounded by hills and lakes and living in a comfortably furnished apartment on a highly desirable private development. It was the kind of affluent America, which I imagine most British people assume to be the norm. There were two entrances to the estate, both with gatehouses, and any visitor was carefully screened before being admitted. This presented me with a problem since I was neither a house owner nor a car owner. Because I did not own property, I could not belong to the exclusive Club with all the privileges that entailed, and without a car, I could not be given any form of identification. When I pointed out that all local clergy, whether they lived on the estate or not, had identity 'stickers' for their cars, and surely I could have one to show at the gate when I was driven home, I was firmly told that did not change the situation. Only automobiles, not people, would be given recognition! I found myself 'on the edge' of the society in which I was to minister.

It is indeed true that the auto rules. Public transportation is very poor except in the large cities, and often the nearest store will be several miles from where people live. When we first discussed my appointment in the parish I explained that I did not hold an English driver's licence, because acute nystagmus made it impossible for me to pass the eye test. However, it seemed that in many American States the testing was less stringent and that I might well obtain a licence or, failing that, I could ride a moped. I found that in New Jersey the eye test was as strict as that in England, and by the time I arrived, a licence was also required for a moped. The only way I could do the job to which I had been appointed was by hiring someone to chauffeur me, and depending on the generosity of parishioners to offer me rides to and from meetings.

I believe that this was a salutary experience for me and for them. I lived more than two miles from the church and four miles from the stores and main highway. There were no sidewalks, which made walking hazardous, and I had to be highly organized, scheduling meetings and appointments well in advance, in order to cope. However, as a clergyperson dependent on the help of those to whom I ministered, a new dimension of priesthood emerged. Parishioners saw that I had needs, that I was not omnicompetent, and that we have gifts to offer one another; driving a car was one such gift. The person who acted as my regular driver was a young widow with three small children. We became good friends and our times together presented many pastoral opportunities and helped her back into the Church.

There were times when I felt angry and frustrated at being so isolated and dependent on others. I was often aware that the more immediate pastoral demands and emergencies had to be dealt with by the Rector because I was not mobile. I felt guilty that I was not taking my share in this ministry, until we talked it through and agreed that I should specifically concentrate on those areas in which I could play a full part. I then established regular hours in the church office, developed Christian Education courses, and concentrated my parish visiting on houses that were close to where I lived.

While I was at St David's, I took part in the usual liturgical and sacramental aspects of ministry, sharing these duties with the Rector. I also became responsible for a weekly house Eucharist. A group of women, most of them with young children, gathered each Friday morning in one of their homes for coffee and discussion. The topics were wide-ranging and very pertinent to their life situation, often dealing with issues of marriage, motherhood, and how to find a relevant spirituality in the midst of family demands. Over the years I have learned to respect women, and value the wisdom they have to offer me, as I have come to appreciate my own womanhood. This group gave me a great deal through their honest sharing of who and what they were, and I believe they were able to be open with me in a way that would not have been possible with a male priest. In the church where I grew up, women's groups were forbidden because the pastor believed nothing good would come of them. Women's meetings were inevitably 'gossip shops' because that was the way women were! It took me many years to realize that I was continuing to trivialize women and unconsciously retaining that negation of who I am.

My visiting of parishioners also brought me into touch with many desperately lonely women, whose lives were empty and meaningless. In terms of material needs they had everything, but time hung heavy on their hands. A visit to the tennis or bridge club, lunch with a friend, a leisurely afternoon, maybe an appointment at the beauty parlour, then occasionally preparing dinner (they tended to eat out many evenings) filled their day. Many were utterly bored, some had become alcoholics, and marriage breakdown was commonplace. Here was a whole area of ministry which I had not anticipated, and one which was as much needed as that which I had expected to be exercising among the poor and oppressed. It took me some time to deal with my own prejudice against such privileged, wealthy members of society, and to recognize that often behind the apparent self-assurance, there was terrible loneliness. I also wanted to resist being regarded as the woman priest, who ministered to women, but to have refused these opportunities would have been to deny any obvious need.

I began to lead an adult class in New Testament studies and enjoyed the exchange of ideas as we applied the biblical material to contemporary life. This also gave me an opportunity to teach again, something I greatly love and had missed since leaving London. From time to time I was invited to preach in other parishes and also spoke at both the Roman Catholic and Episcopal cathedrals of the diocese. Often it was because I was from England and because people knew of my ordination that the invitations were offered. I responded by agreeing to preach on the 'propers' for the day, saying that I was not prepared to come and talk about women priests or my own experience. At a number of informal meetings I did agree to discuss these topics, but I have grown increasingly reluctant to do so. I want to be accepted as a priest with a priestly ministry to offer and not simply as a symbol or exhibit.

All the clergy of Kinnelon met together for breakfast each week in an effort to share resources and promote ecumenical endeavour. There were representatives of the Roman Catholic, Presbyterian, Methodist, United Reformed and Episcopal churches. We held joint services on such occasions as Thanksgiving, and ran a combined Vacation Bible School for the children during the summer.

Sunday was, of course, a very busy day for the clergy at St David's. Services took place at 8 a.m. and 10 a.m. and then there was a coffee hour which provided an opportunity to meet informally with people and often to set up appointments for interviews later in the week. One of the things I especially appreciated was the fact that my vestments were designed and made by members of the parish. For my ordination one parishioner made a red chasuble with a descending white dove on the front — symbol of the Holy Spirit and also of St David — and gold flames on the back. A green chasuble was made by another member of the parish, this time the design depicting growth and new life, and a third, white one, was completed just in time for my first Easter celebration.

Kinnelon is thirty-five miles from New York City and I took the bus each Wednesday at noon, and stayed overnight at the Seminary, where I was taking the Spiritual Direction course. Classes were all day on Thursday. It was good to meet up again with Kath Burn, a friend from England who, like me, had tired of waiting for the Church of England to test her vocation to the priesthood. She was then completing the final year of her training in America, hoping one day to return as a priest to the land where she had become aware of her call. I loved being in New York, sometimes taking time off to visit a theatre or art gallery, and meeting with people, who shared my concern to explore and develop spiritual life. The course offered a historical perspective on spiritual direction, study of the classical Christian texts, supervised work with directees, the study and practice of different forms of prayer, and psychological insights into human growth and development. Previously I had used my counselling training and personal experience of being in spiritual direction, as I worked with others pursuing their spiritual journey. Now a variety of models of spiritual direction were explored, and support given to all of us preparing to be better equipped for this ministry.

Back in the parish I invited any who would like to work with me in spiritual direction to contact me. I soon learned that many were hungry for just this kind of help as they tried to make sense of their own spiritual journey. In a short space of time I had a number of parishioners as well as some seminarians, meeting with me on a regular basis. Of course, any case histories presented for discussion in small group seminars, were completely anonymous and only offered with the agreement of the directees. A thesis, commitment to receiving regular spiritual direction, and attendance at four retreats during the two years are further requirements of the course.

At the beginning of September 1982 I moved to an apartment at the Seminary. In addition to completing the STM Course I teach courses offered by the Center for Christian Spirituality in a programme designed to bring together clergy and laity in the metropolitan area for study and reflection. I work with small groups in spiritual direction, encouraging shared exploration and support in the spiritual pilgrimage. I also serve a large city parish, offering seminars and retreats and specializing in spirituality there.

Where will the future lie? I am uncertain — life is still being lived 'at the edge'. I have an increasing number of retreats and workshops scheduled for the next year in the USA and England. I believe that God is calling me to continue to be available for this ministry wherever it may be. I welcome invitations to work with parishes, retreat centres and other groups and I sense a deep hunger for spiritual growth among many who find themselves at the very margins of the institutional Church as well as among those within it.

Ultimately whether or not we perceive ourselves as standing 'at the edge' depends on our perspective. The edge is sometimes dangerous but it is also often the place where real movement takes place. I am reminded of some words by Dorothee Sölle:

> But first we must accept the fact of our historical situation. It is not the centre from which liberation will come; it comes from the periphery. Christ was not born in the palace of Herod but in a stable. He did not grow up in the centre of Jewish culture among the power élite but in the backwaters of Galilee.[2]

As I consider the life of Jesus, his healing, forgiving, life-enhancing proclamation of God's truth, I find his edge to be the centre of reality. And I hear in the gospel an invitation to risk going there with him, even when it means a loss of security, because only there will I find freedom to live authentically. The centre is where I find Christ crucified and risen, and that often seems to be at the margins of Church and Society.

9 Reflections

Writing an autobiography is a difficult task. As we tell our personal story we bump up against reticence, for we are putting on record the self-realization of our unconscious, and this process is incomplete. Although we may partially direct the psychic process, we cannot control it and we have no objective foundation from which to judge ourselves. The best we can do is to tell *our* truth as honestly as possible, and trust in the charitableness of our readers.

When he finally agreed to allow his memories, dreams and reflections to be recorded for posterity, C. G. Jung claimed that the only events in his life worth telling were those, 'when the imperishable world erupted into this transitory one'.[1] This was why he included dreams and visions and believed that outward circumstances were no substitute for inner experience. I have tried to include in this account of my pilgrimage something of my inner journey, a journey which continues. I thank God for every occasion when I have recognized the inbreaking of the Other, generating new energy and broadening my vision.

I am a priest. That is the single, most definitive fact of my life. During this year since the Church set her seal upon my vocation I have reflected on what priesthood means to me. My reflections are not complete but I offer them here because they are an important part of who I am and of what I am becoming.

For centuries masculine values have been dominant and this has had a powerful effect on women's psyche. Man has tended to despise his 'inferior', 'feminine' side and woman has learned to despise her own dominant value, the femininity which is at the centre of her being. Even after she has consciously changed this attitude, it persists in the unconscious. Thus many women project on to trivial vanities or domestic activity the despised feminine values. Womanhood then becomes identified with a despised aspect of man's anima. Inevitably this year has involved much searching and pondering on what it means to be a woman and a priest. There is always the danger in this kind of situation that women will work in imitation of men instead of out of their own natures, and thus become identified with an inferior kind of masculinity. In a reaction against age-long degradation of the feminine, women have demanded equality with men on the level of value and ability so that they might find freedom from the contempt which has tried to confine them to conventional roles. However, this has sometimes been attempted by trying to obliterate all difference between the sexes, and has resulted in an even worse kind of contempt. In the process one half of reality has been rejected and the individual woman has become submerged into the meaninglessness of imitation. The true freedom and creativeness of woman is lost.

I do not like being referred to as a 'woman priest'. I am a priest who happens to be a woman and I bring my whole personhood to that ministry. However, I do recognize that there are aspects of the priesthood and of God which become more clearly visible to me when I see a woman celebrate the Eucharist. Defining them is more difficult. On two occasions when I have been celebrant a man from the congregation has spoken to me afterwards of his sense of being nourished and nurtured as he received communion. The stylized liturgy with a male president obscured the fact that we were celebrating a meal together; this dimension was recovered as a woman was seen doing what women most often do: preparing, serving and cleaning up after a meal. I am not entirely comfortable with this kind of projection, but I am aware that centuries of theological and confessional interpretation have obscured the original context of the institution of the Eucharist.

It seems to me that women are, in a special way, carriers of relatedness. The ministry of reconciliation which we proclaim as priests is one in which women are constantly engaged. In the home as mother and wife; in the business world as employer and colleague; in the Church, dealing with the claims of diverse groups. Women seem to have a heightened capacity to make connections between theology and life. I think of a thoroughly pragmatic theologian, like Dorothee Sölle, and of the many times I have heard a woman at a clergy conference offer exactly the word which enabled polarized opinions to meet creatively.

Intuition- and feeling-values are also important to the priesthood. It is a commonplace to say that these are more highly developed in women, and a gross over-simplification. Nevertheless, my observations are that women clergy have especially been agents for enabling others, male clergy and parishioners, to own and celebrate these aspects of their being. My work in liturgical dance has been an important aspect of priesthood, for it has not only been a means of enabling participants to release feeling and emotion in worship, but of expressing my own offering of body and spirit as well as mind to God.

As soon as we try to define 'masculine' or 'feminine' qualities, we run into difficulty, and the attempt to categorize too rigidly is inappropriate. I once observed a woman priest kneeling to give the blessing to small children at the communion rail, because she wanted very much to meet them at eye level and express welcome and warmth. What a typically feminine sensitivity, I thought. Then I saw my bishop assume the same posture at a large Cathedral Eucharist!

I have no clear answer to the question, 'What does it mean to be a woman and a priest?' All I know is that I have to offer the whole of what I am to God for this ministry, and that includes my femininity. I also know that when I see a woman presiding at the Eucharist, I feel that my own priesthood and womanhood is being affirmed. It is for this reason, and because of the deep pastoral needs I have encountered in England, that I continue to celebrate the Eucharist, and to give the blessing and absolution to those who yearn for women's priestly ministry. I also long for the day when the gender of the priest ceases to matter because men and women are equally accepted.

Thoughts of England lead me to another aspect of my experience as a priest; it has meant exile. In order to be true to my vocation it was necessary to leave friends, home and country, learning to live hopefully in a new land. I learned something about exile from Bishop Colin Winter. Expelled from Namibia, because he refused to implement the inhuman policies of apartheid in his diocese, he worked tirelessly in London, establishing the Namibia International Peace Centre as a haven for refugees, and became deeply involved in working for the poor and powerless people of the East End. As 'Bishop of Namibia in Exile' he was marginalized by the Church because of his outspoken, uncompromising and prophetic witness. He was a man of deep compassion, who reached out in solidarity to me as I contemplated leaving for America. Though he yearned for Namibia, Colin lived positively in the present, recognizing that exile can be a place of renewed vision, creative energy and hope. His awareness of the strength and tenacity found in women of faith, led him to compose a litany in praise of their testimony, and printed in *Celebration for a Prioress* in June 1981.[2]

I went into exile and, like the people of Israel in Babylon who longed for Jerusalem, I often found myself longing for the land and the Church in which my vocation had grown. The lament of Psalm 137 was often pertinent to my sense of loss:

> By the waters of Babylon, there we sat down and wept,
> when we remembered Zion.
> On the willows there we hung up our lyres . . .
> How shall we sing the Lord's song in a foreign land?

But I also found, as they did, that the 'far country' was alive with the presence of God and this led to new perceptions of that reality. There have been those like Jeremiah and Ezekiel who have encouraged and inspired me. I have made many good friends and discovered a new community of faith. It would seem that out of the Babylonian exile synagogue worship developed and a renewal of the inner core of religious faith took place for the exiles deprived of the temple in Jerusalem. So for me there has been a challenge to define what is really central in my believing and a joy at the discovery of new dimensions of faith. In America I have found a vitality and openness among Christians, a recognition of my priesthood, an affirmation of my ministry. The place of exile has been a life-enhancing and hope-filled land, full of the presence of God.

I have also learned that to be a priest means to be a symbol. For the first few months after ordination, I exhausted myself trying to live up to the many different expectations people placed upon me. There is a real sense in which any priest becomes a 'public' person but this was heightened in my case by the media interest in my ordination. Some saw me as a hopeful sign of freedom for women; others as a confrontational challenge to the church. Mary Kenny writing in the *Daily Mail,* 21 December 1981, considered that my hairstyle and lipstick rendered me an unsuitable candidate for priesthood! (Others are 'put off' by women priests who do not look 'feminine' enough.) I quickly learned that women priests are judged by what people see or experience in one woman. My word or action could prove decisive for the person not yet convinced about women and the priesthood. This is a feature much less pronounced where male priests are concerned.

There were those who had been friends but could not deal with the public nature of my ordination and so began to withdraw their support. I no longer met their expectations or gave them undivided attention. There were times, especially during December 1981 and January 1982, when I felt like the quarry hunted down by a pack of hounds and torn into many pieces. I needed friends to be patient with me, to go on loving me when I felt fragmented and tired, and as I tried to adjust to a new role. Some did that with enormous tolerance and compassion. My spiritual director offered some timely wisdom when I expressed my frustration about the pressure of living up to diverse expectations and of being a symbol to so many. He pointed out that there was no way to escape the projections which people placed upon me for this was an inevitable part of my vocation given the historical situation in which I found myself and the pioneer nature of what I had done. But *I did not have to take up any of those images for myself.* I needed to be me, a priest and a person, maintaining my integrity, making the best of all that came my way. This was a liberating insight for me. Criticism still hurts. I am uncomfortable when people say I should be more radical or less so; when they ask me to do things which I know will lead to misunderstanding or when they tell me to fade into anonymity. But I am becoming able to offer who and what I am to God more fully, to risk sometimes being wrong and to leave the consequences with the only One to whom they matter ultimately. I refuse to live up to the myth of omnicompetence.

I have long believed that servanthood, not paternalism, best serves as an image of priesthood. This year has meant addressing the question at several levels. First, I am a little worried when I hear women denying any interest in 'status' as priests saying they simply want to be demonstrating the servant role. My concern arises from the fact that women have been perceived as offering a supportive servant ministry for so long that we need other images. Yet I do not want to adopt a traditional paternalistic stance in which an invulnerable cleric is set apart from other Christians as an authoritarian leader. It is important to recognize the authority of women priests — this is not the same as authoritarianism — but also to appreciate our desire to serve the Body of Christ by enabling others to recognize and release their gifts for ministry. How do these two aspects of priesthood come together?

Even in America, though many women are highly skilled and experienced as priests, they do not easily find appointments as rectors of parishes. First jobs and curacies are available, but somehow when it comes to appointing a woman as the leader of a congregation, prejudice asserts itself. We are still caught up in the servant image; it is appropriate for women to be assistants, but even the most radical parish is less certain about hiring a woman rector.

One indication that there remain unresolved questions about women in the priesthood is that we have still not decided what to call them! My personal preference is that people use my first name — my baptismal name — rather than a title. However, I recognize that many are very uncomfortable with this and it is important to respect their sensitivity. 'Reverend' will not do (though it is a very common form of address for men and women clergy in the USA). I like 'sister', but that too is inappropriate as long as men are 'father', since it reinforces inequality. In a context where 'father' is the usual form of address I have accepted the title 'mother', not because I think it is ideal, but because the parent relationship is capable of reinterpretation. I react negatively to 'father' used when believers are kept in childish dependence on the prohibitions or permissions of the priest. Those who understand good parenting enable their children to grow up into independence; they help them to take risks, allow them to make mistakes, and provide a loving environment in which dialogue can take place. As long as the priest exercises her/his parenting in a way which enables people to grow to maturity in Christ the title 'mother' or 'father' may be appropriate. I have not yet discovered a suitable non-sexist replacement.

Status is important, and is not to be confused with power (though the two do seem to be synonymous in the hierarchy of the Church). It has been suggested that women should not concern themselves with wanting status as priests, that they can do almost all the things men do, that they should thus feel fulfilled in their ministry. Strangely, I have never heard the same statement addressed to men seeking ordination! It has been important for me to know that the Church has recognized my vocation and made plain my status as a priest. I no longer live only with an inner personal conviction that this is what I am; the Church has tested, affirmed, and publicly recognized that status. It has confirmed my authority to celebrate the Holy Eucharist and to pronounce the blessing and absolution in Christ's name.

Being a priest has also meant being a catalyst. Things have happened as a result of my ordination. Some of them have been the cause of rejoicing, others have been painful. I am reminded often of the struggle which took place in the New Testament era as traditional Jewish believers wrestled to allow their monotheism to be expanded by their experience of Jesus Christ and the Spirit, and as they came to see Gentiles in a new light. The acceptance by the Church of non-Jewish Christians without their submission to circumcision and other Jewish laws, was an issue on which people were divided for many years. The tension is revealed in the Epistles and its divisive nature told in vivid story form in the book of Acts. Of particular importance is Acts 10.1 — 11.18, because it contains a detailed apology by which Peter justified his attitude before the Jewish Christians in Jerusalem. It is later cited before the 'Apostolic' council as decisive evidence that the Gentiles are accepted by God (Acts 15).

I believe this change in tradition provides us with a close parallel to the acceptance of women as priests in the Church today. It was a hard-won victory which continued to trouble those who would not allow their convictions to expand. According to Gal. 2.11, even Peter had second thoughts and was challenged by Paul to be consistent! Fortunately they did not wait for everyone to agree before taking action on what seemed clearly to be God's purpose. The ordination of women — my ordination — has been divisive. Some people have been compelled to face their uncertainty and have reacted with anger or withdrawn support. The question to be asked is whether division is necessarily wrong. My reading of the gospel and my understanding of the ministry of Jesus leads me to the belief that it is inevitable, and that honestly dealing with it can be creative. At the end of his offensive discourse about eating his flesh and drinking his blood Jesus lost friends: 'After this many of his disciples drew back and no longer went about with him' (John 6.66).

Those who stayed, and who faced the difficult questions they could not yet answer, learned from him what eternal life meant.

Being a priest means learning to live with paradox. As a priest I am to be a focus of unity, of the reconciliation and acceptance which God offers through me to all humankind. In the words of St Francis I am to be an 'instrument of peace' bringing harmony where there is discord, love where there is hatred, pardon where there is injury. Yet it is also the task of the priest to challenge, to proclaim truth however unpalatable, to be a prophetic witness in the world. And that divides; it brings not peace but a sword. The one thing I must do is to go on loving those who turn back or reject what I am. I must go on forgiving just as I trust those whom I injure to find the charity to forgive me my insensitivity to their pain.

A year is a short time in which to learn what priesthood means. I am still a beginner, still discovering new dimensions to this ministry, still overwhelmed by an awesome sense of the privilege and responsibility of my vocation. I am grateful to all who have supported me through their prayers, challenged me with their honesty, sustained me by their love. The Order of Service for my ordination contained the prayer of Charles de Foucauld and I invited people to use it as a focus for meditation while they waited for the service to begin. It is a prayer I find devastating in its simplicity. It scares me to utter those words, yet I try to go on saying them to a totally loving God who invites me to intimacy and who holds in being all I am and all I shall be.

> Father,
>
> I abandon myself into your hands;
> do with me what you will.
> Whatever you may do, I thank you:
> I am ready for all, I accept all.
>
> Let only your will be done in me,
> And in all your creatures.
> I wish no more than this, O Lord.
>
> Into your hands I commend my soul;
> I offer it to you
> With all the love in my heart,
> for I love you, Lord,
> and so need to give myself,
> to surrender myself into your hands,
> without reserve,
> and with boundless confidence,
>
> for you are my Father.

Appendix 1
The Deaconess Order

At the end of the nineteenth century there was a movement to restore the ancient ministry of deaconesses in the Church and those like Bishop Lightfoot who pioneered the cause, claimed scriptural authority for doing so. Although there is ambiguity about some of the New Testament references to women who served in the capacity of a 'diakonos' (the Greek word for deacon is of common gender), the evidence suggests that in at least some parts of the early church there was a recognized female diaconate. Throughout the centuries which followed, the Church in both East and West recognized deaconesses, sometimes investing them with considerable authority — some abbesses who were deaconesses were given quasi-episcopal status — and at others making clear their subordination to the male diaconate. As time went by, deaconesses were largely replaced by nuns, partly because their specific duties with regard to women at baptism were lessened as the rite changed, but also because rapid expansion of religious orders provided new ways for women to serve the church.

Industrial expansion, and the rapid urbanization of the nineteenth century, resulted in vast numbers of poor tenement dwellers living in squalour and a prey to sickness. In an attempt to reach these 'unchurched' masses, women were called upon in a variety of ways, and various houses and communities of workers established. However, it was not until 1862 that Bishop Tait ordained Elizabeth Catherine Ferard as deaconess, the first woman since the Reformation to be so recognized. The new foundation to which she belonged became the Deaconess Community of St Andrew, and its purpose was to restore the ancient order of deaconesses in the Church of England. Nursing, teaching, and training women for domestic service were among the activities of the Sisters (a title retained even after ordination as a deaconess). The number of women seeking to become deaconesses increased throughout the country, some also embracing the religious life, and in 1871 General Principles and Rules were formulated to give them official recognition. Eighteen bishops and the two archbishops signed this document.

A new emphasis in the movement came from the Rochester diocese where Deaconess Isabella Gilmore was appointed Head of the Rochester Deaconess Institution. Here practical training was given, but theological study was also required, with a final examination after two years of training, and before ordination. The Institution was soon sending trained deaconesses out to other Dioceses. In 1891 the Upper House of the Convocation of Canterbury passed Resolutions on deaconesses as follows:

That Deaconesses, having according to the best authorities, formed an order of ministry in the early Church, and having proved their efficiency in the Anglican Church, it is desirable to encourage the formation of Deaconess Institutions and the work of Deaconesses in our dioceses and parishes.

2   That a Deaconess should be admitted in solemn form by the Bishop, with benediction, by laying on of hands.

3   That there should be an adequate term of preparation and probation.

4   That a Deaconess so admitted may be released from her obligations by the Bishop of the diocese in which she was admitted, if he think fit, on cause shown.

5   That no Deaconess should be admitted to serve in any parish without a licence from the Bishop of the diocese, given at the request of the Incumbent or Curate-in-charge.

6   That the dress of Deaconesses should be simple, but distinctive.

7   That a Deaconess should not pass from one diocese to another without the written permission of both Bishops.

8   That special care should be taken to provide for every Deaconess sufficient time and opportunity for the strengthening of her own spiritual life.

These guidelines indicated a concern that deaconesses relate closely to the bishop, and that women's ministry be seen to be clearly within the establishment. Although deaconesses seem always to have been admitted to the office by episcopal imposition of hands, no clarity is offered about the rite used. There were some objections raised to this practice by members of Convocation who feared it might make the status of a deaconess analagous to that of a deacon! There were also differences of understanding concerning the permanence or otherwise of the office. The uncertainty about the status of deaconesses was undoubtably a contributory factor to the increase in numbers of lay workers serving the Church.

The women's movement, and especially the cause of women's suffrage, was welcomed and embraced by some of the deaconesses, and in 1912 the Church League for Women's Suffrage was formed. This led to further pressure to admit women to the diaconate and by 1915 Miss Maude Royden was even suggesting women might be priests! Her request that women be allowed to speak in church was met with limited approval by two bishops, provided that precise conditions were observed (the Bishop of London made it clear that a woman might not speak from pulpit, lectern or chancel steps). Even this limited concession evoked vehement opposition and the columns of the *Church Times* were filled with protest, much of it from the English Church Union. So vociferous were the objectors that the Bishop rescinded his earlier permission for women to speak in church.

The First World War saw many women assuming roles which would previously have been unthinkable, and it led to change in the general status of women in British society. These changes were reflected in the resolutions proposed by the Lambeth Conference meeting in 1920.

'47   The time has come, when, in the interests of the Church at large, and in particular of the development of the Ministry of Women, the Diaconate of Women should be restored formally and canonically, and should be recognised throughout the Anglican Communion.

48   The Order of Deaconesses is for women the one and only Order of the Ministry which has the stamp of Apostolic approval, and is for women the only Order of Ministry which we can recommend that our Branch of the Catholic Church should recogonize and use.

49   The office of a Deaconess is primarily a ministry of succour, bodily and spiritual, especially to women, and should follow the lines of the primitive rather than of the modern Diaconate of men. It should be understood that the Deaconess dedicates herself to a lifelong service, but that no vow or implied promise of celibacy should be required as necessary for admission to the Order. Nevertheless, Deaconesses who desire to do so may legitimately pledge themselves either as members of a Community, or as individuals, to a celibate life.

50   In every branch of the Anglican Communion there should be adopted a Form and Manner of Making of Deaconesses such as might fitly find a place in the Book of Common Prayer, containing in all cases provision for:

a. Prayer by the bishop and the laying on of his hands;
b. A formula giving authority to execute the Office of a deacon in the Church of God.

51   The Forms for the Making and Ordering of Deaconesses should be of the same general character, and as far as possible similar in their most significant parts, though varying in less important details in accordance with local needs.

52   The following functions may be entrusted to the Deaconess, in addition to the ordinary duties which would naturally fall to her:

a. To prepare candidates for Baptism and Confirmation;
b. To assist at the administration of Holy Baptism; and to be the administrant in cases of necessity in virtue of her office;
c. To pray with and to give counsel to such women as desire help in difficulties and perplexities;
d. With the approval of the Bishop and of the Parish Priest, and under such conditions as shall from time to time be laid down by the Bishop:

    i. in Church to read Morning and Evening Prayer and the Litany, except such portions as are assigned to the Priest only;

    ii. in Church also to lead in prayer and, under licence of the Bishop, to instruct and exhort the Congregation.'

It was suggested that if the Church did not adequately recognize the ministry of women, there would be a great wastage of gifts because many able women would feel alienated from the Church and the faith. However, other Provinces of the Anglican Communion were far more prepared to act on the Lambeth Resolutions than the Mother Church and once again a barrage of protest, especially over the suggestion that women might be in holy orders, was unleashed. The English Church Union, and several other bodies, organized petitions against such outrage.

In her excellent survey of the Deaconess Order, Janet Grierson quotes a letter she received from Dss. Ethel Chapman, who was ordained in 1927. It closely approximates to my own feeling of ambivalence about becoming a deaconess:

> Exploration revealed that the deaconess order was not a popular way of service, and was both limited and open to a very great deal of prejudice and misunderstanding. Many of the more militant women desiring opportunities for service in the Church looked upon the Deaconess Order as a hindrance to their aspirations and efforts. Nevertheless, in obedience to my call I offered myself for ordination. The Church offered no other way. She did offer *this.* I saw my ordination as an opportunity to commit myself to life-long service to Christ and His Church and upon it the Church set the seal of her acceptance and blessing.[1]

The Lambeth Conference of 1930 did little to remove the ambiguities of the Order and, in fact, made explicit the difference between deaconess and deacon, even removing the clause, '. . . which has the stamp of Apostolic approval', from the 1920 Resolution. The voice of those who were pressing for the ordination of women to the priesthood was also being raised more clearly at this time especially through the agency of such bodies as the Society for the Ministry of Women and the Anglican Group for the Ordination of Women.

It was not until 1964 that Royal Assent was given to Canons on Deaconesses (D.1—3), though subsequent revision quickly became necessary when the function of Lay Readers was established in the Church of England. The latter included women and no restrictions were made about preaching at Holy Communion, so deaconesses found themselves at a disadvantage. A drastic revision of Canon D.1. was approved in 1973, removing the restriction on preaching and adding some liturgical functions.

The Lambeth Conference of 1968 recommended that women who had been made deaconesses by the laying-on-of-hands and appropriate prayer be declared to be within the diaconate. This recommendation was made in the context of much debate about the nature of the diaconate (including the possibility of a permanent diaconate for men and women), and of the ordination of women to the priesthood. Although it was not implemented in the Church of England, other Provinces did recognise deaconesses in this way: Kenya, Korea, Canada, 1968; USA, 1970; New Zealand, 1972; Uganda, 1973; Japan, 1974; and Central Africa, 1976. In England continued debate about the ordination of women to the priesthood led to a shelving of the question of recognition of deaconesses as deacons within the threefold orders of ministry.

In 1971 the Ministry Committee of the Accredited Council for the Church's Ministry set up a working party to discuss the Resolutions of the Lambeth Conference. Two reports were issued: *Deacons in the Church* (1974) and three years later, *The Ministry of Deacons and Deaconesses,* and these prepared the way for further discussion of the matter at General Synod in 1977. During that debate Deaconess Joan Diment made the following statement:

> At the present time deaconesses do not know who they are and their congregations do not know who they are, and upon this uncertainty rests many an unsatisfactory and unrewarding ministry. Upon it rests a debilitating uncertainty, wasteful of a deaconess's potential powers, and an insecurity which can generate disillusionment and heartbreak.[2]

During the last few years progress has been made in some areas.

Appendix 1

Some deaconesses hold responsible jobs in administration, chaplaincy, and diocesan appointments, and a few have charge of parishes. In churches where they are employed, many more liturgical functions are open to them than in the past, so that congregations have some experience of ordained women's ministry. But there are wide areas where lay people have never ever seen a woman in the sanctuary, and a good deal of education is still needed. As I write, the General Synod has given approval for preparation of legislation which would open the diaconate to women (the Church in Wales has already done so). It remains to be seen whether this will receive approval when the final vote is taken.

Over eighty years ago the first bishop of Birmingham, Charles Gore, said during a sermon in Westminster Abbey:

> The Order of Deaconesses has not yet the same position in the Church as that of Deacons, but it only waits for the Church to take formal action on its behalf.

It still waits! Janet Grierson records the following statement by Archbishop Davidson made in his address to the Head Deaconess Association in 1908:

> . . . the time had not yet come when it would be wise to get an opinion from the Bishops as to deaconess work, life, training etc. A longer experimental stage is necessary before it would be wise to work for legal enactments. The Deaconesses must prove their usefulness to the Church by quiet work, for some years to come, and wait until by this means their work and position be better known and recognized.[3]

Perhaps some of those women, who have gone on quietly serving the Church as deaconesses for thirty or forty years, can be forgiven for asking, 'How long, O Lord?'

Appendix 2

A brief historical survey
of the ordination of women as priests
in the Anglican Communion

The first ordination of a woman to the priesthood in the Anglican Communion took place in 1944. A shortage of priests, and a recognition of the competence and calling of Deaconess Lee Tim Oi, led Bishop R. O. Hall of Hong Kong and South China to ordain her to serve as priest on the island of Macao. Two years later the bishops of the Chinese Anglican Church discussed this action, and the diocese proposed that a canon which would permit the ordination of a deaconess to the priesthood, be enacted. This was referred to the Lambeth Conference of 1948 which decided that such an experiment would be against Anglican tradition and order, and concluded that the time had not yet come for further consideration of the issue. It was reported that the Revd Lee Tim Oi had resigned her orders, though she has since denied that this was so.

At the next Lambeth Conference it was noted that women were being adequately trained and were coming forward for work in the Church. No further action was taken, however, beyond a recommendation that trained women workers be more fully employed, especially in areas of pioneer work. A cautious statement was issued at the Conference of 1968:

> The Conference affirms its opinion that the theological arguments as at present presented for and against the ordination of women to the priesthood are inconclusive.

However, there was a request that each Province of the Anglican Communion give careful study to the subject, and prepare a report of findings for the next meeting of the Anglican Consultative Council.

Appendix 2

In 1971 the ACC met in Kenya and, although not all the requested reports were presented, passed a Resolution that all Churches of the Anglican Communion should give consideration to the ordination of women by 1973. It further requested all metropolitans and primates in the Anglican Communion to consult with other Churches in their areas and advised the Bishop of Hong Kong that if, with the approval of his Synod, he decided to ordain women to the priesthood, this would be acceptable to the Council. Any other bishop of the Anglican Communion acting with the approval of his Province might do likewise and the Council would use its good offices to encourage all Provinces of the Anglican Communion to continue in communion with such dioceses. Later that year the Bishop of Hong Kong ordained two more women to the priesthood and further ordinations took place in 1973 and 1976.

The General Convention of the Episcopal Church in the USA (ECUSA) voted against the ordination of women to the priesthood at its triennial meeting in 1973. This decision was effected by a vote in the House of Deputies (clergy and laity) though the Bishops were in favour and had, in the previous year, affirmed their belief in the ordination of women at the House of Bishops Meeting. Pressure for change had been increasing, especially since women had been ordained to the diaconate, and this was not the first 'No' decision in that Church. Anticipating a wait of at least three years before the question could be raised again, three Bishops irregularly ordained eleven women as priests in Philadelphia. A year later four more women were ordained in Washington, DC. In September 1976 the General Convention voted for the ordination of women to the priesthood and the fifteen women who had been irregularly ordained were regularized. They were not re-ordained.

A year before America formally approved the ordination of women, the General Synod of the Anglican Church in Canada re-affirmed the rightness of ordaining women and stated that it would be appropriate for suitably qualified women to be ordained at 'the discretion of the diocesan bishops acting within the normal

107

procedures of their own jurisdictions and in consultation with the House of Bishops'.

The voting was as follows:

	IN FAVOUR	AGAINST
Laity	95	9
Clergy	86	19
Bishops	27	7
	208	35

Archbishop Scott, on a visit to England, suggested that the long history of women engaged in pioneer work communicating the gospel in isolated rural areas, and a careful period of study and open discussion of the issue, led to the massive vote in favour of women priests and a comparatively trouble-free transition period. The first six women were ordained to the priesthood in the Anglican Church of Canada in November 1976.

In May 1976 the General Synod of the Church of the Province of New Zealand made a final decision to ordain women to the priesthood. Again there was a substantial majority.

The voting was as follows:

	IN FAVOUR	AGAINST
Bishops	6	1
Clergy	17	5
Laity	23	2
	46	8

Five women were ordained to the priesthood in New Zealand in December 1977.

The General Synod of the Church of England debated in 1975 the Motion:

That this Synod considers that there are no fundamental objections to the ordination of women to the priesthood.

Appendix 2

The motion was carried by a substantial majority:

	AYES	NOES	ABSTENTIONS
Bishops	28	10	0
Clergy	110	96	2
Laity	117	74	3
	255	180	5

but a further Motion to remove 'the legal and other barriers' was defeated.

When the Lambeth Conference met in 1978 it recommended that the autonomy of member Churches should be recognized, and unity within the Anglican Communion maintained. It declared its acceptance of both the Provinces which had ordained women to the priesthood and those which had not. In July the General Synod met again and voted against removing the legal barriers to the ordination of women. The Motion was lost.

	AYES	NOES
Bishops	32	17
Clergy	94	149
Laity	120	106

A year later a Motion calling for temporary legislation to allow legally ordained women priests from other Anglican Provinces to officiate during visits to England was also lost in spite of an overall majority of 35 in favour:

	AYES	NOES
Bishops	26	10
Clergy	87	113
Laity	110	65

A similar Motion, approved during the July 1982 General Synod, (and discussed in chapter 7 of this book) led to a decision to prepare legislation which would allow women to function as priests in a limited way during visits to England. This legislation will then require a vote, probably two-thirds majority in each House, to effect change.

In 1981 the General Synod of the Anglican Church of Australia approved a canon to prepare the way for the ordination of women to the priesthood. Several other Churches or Provinces of the Anglican Communion have agreed in principle to the ordination of women to the priesthood. Some have decided against and several have made no response.

A number of useful pamphlets and publications on this issue are available from:

The Movement for the Ordination of Women,
Napier Hall, Hyde Place, Vincent Street,
London SW1P 4NJ

Two important booklets published by the Church Information Office are also available: *The Ordination of Women to the Priesthood* (GS. 104) 1972; *The Ordination of Women: Supplement to GS. 104* (GS. Misc:88) 1978.

Appendix 3

'Celebration for a Prioress'

ANTIPHON
There were also women looking on from afar, among whom were Mary Magdalene, and Mary, the mother of James the younger and of Joseph, and Salome, who, when he was in Galilee, followed him and ministered to him; and also many other women who came up with him to Jerusalem: (Mark 15.40)
Alleluia!

V Sarah, our mother, foundress of the new-born creation, who laughed in disbelieving joy at God's plan for you.

R Come and stand here among us.

V Deborah, prophetess and judge, who rallied the people against their oppressors.

R Come and stand here among us.

V Hannah, who sang your heart out to the God of liberation.

R Come and stand here among us.

V Ruth, faithful in suffering and in poverty, grandmother of King David, who shows us there are no outcasts with God.

R Come and stand here among us.

V Mary, the mother of Jesus, exultant with joy in bearing him, unflinching at his side in death.

R Come and stand here among us.

V Mary of Magdala, pouring out your love like perfume for him, witness of his resurrection.

R Come and stand here among us.

V Clare, lover of the poor, fellow worker with Francis.

R Come and stand here among us.

V Catherine, nagger of God, rewarded with visions.

R Come and stand here among us.

V Julian, who saw God's creative hand in a hazel nut and taught us to understand, 'All things will be very well'.

R Come and stand here among us.

V Myrtha, struggling with the oppressed in Chile.

R We will stand beside you.

V Phyllis, crusader for freedom, whose home was bomb-blasted by a South African parcel bomb.

R We will stand beside you.

V Winnie Mandela, whose unshakable faith and courage keeps hope aflame in the hearts of South Africa's oppressed ones.

R We will stand beside you.

V Helen Joseph, banned, silenced, mocked, inspirer of exploited workers and expectant youth.

R We will stand beside you.

V Elizabeth ja Toivo, eighty years a victim of oppression, chosen by God to be mother of Namibia's liberator.

R We will stand beside you.

V Coretta Scott King, peace worker, uncrushed by racist violence.

R We will stand beside you.

V Elizabeth, sharer of our work and exile.

R We will stand beside you.

V Donatella, exposer of hypocrisy and bogus religious posturing.

R We will stand beside you.

V Hannah, with eighty-two years of Cockney humour.

R We will stand beside you.

V Anne and Molly, found guilty of waging peace for wishing to hammer rocket nose cones into ploughshares in America.

R We will stand beside you.

COLIN O'BRIEN WINTER

Notes

Chapter 1   *Surprised by Joy*

1   Lewis C.S., *Surprised by Joy.* London, Fontana, 1959.
2   See Appendix 1, The Deaconess Order.
3   Heyward C., *A Priest Forever* (New York, Harper and Row 1976) p. 32.

Chapter 3   *The Ministry of Reconciliation*

1   Lessing D., *This Was The Old Chief's Country.* 2nd edn, London, Michael Joseph, 1973.
2   Elphinstone A., *Freedom, Suffering and Love* (London, SCM 1976) pp. 8—9.
3   Heyward C., *A Priest Forever* (New York, Harper and Row 1976) p. 32.

Chapter 5   *Ordination*

1   Kairos: A Greek word meaning the opportune or seasonable time, the decisive moment.

Chapter 6   *Walls of Jericho*

1   Allen M. and Elder M., *The Walls of Jericho* (London, BBC Publications 1981) p. 62.

Chapter 8   *At the Edge*

1   Berrigan D., *America is Hard to Find* (London, SPCK 1973) p. 75.
2   Sölle D., 'Radical Religion' (*Christians for Socialism,* 4, 3—4) p. 17.

Chapter 9   *Reflections*

1   Jung C. G., *Memories, Dreams and Reflections* (New York, Vintage Books 1961) p. 4.
2   See Appendix 3.

Appendix 1

1   Grierson J., *The Deaconess* (London, C.I.O. 1981) p. 57.
2   Ibid., p. 116.
3   Ibid., p. 38.